MW00389386

Praise for *The Inside Gig*

"This book is worth its weight in gold even if you only take the questions at the end of each chapter, gather your colleagues and talk about the ones that pop for you. Turn even a few of their very thoughtful takeaways into action and you will be well on your way to readying your organization for the future."

—Beverly Kaye, PhD, author, speaker, consultant; coauthor of *Help Them Grow or Watch Them Go* and *Love 'Em or Lose 'Em*

"Goldberg and Steven-Waiss have sounded the alarm. It's time for companies to recognize people's whole talent and skills. They outline how to remove the barriers, dispel the silos and unlock a skills-based, mobile workforce from inside your company to meet the needs of the future."

—David Blake, coauthor of *Expertise Economy* and cofounder of Degreed

"The future of work looks dramatically different over the next decade and even in the next year. Disruptive technologies, big data, demographic shifts and demand for new skills will require new ways of thinking about careers and preparing a workforce for tomorrow. *The Inside Gig* is infused with the wisdom of leading CHROs, and addresses these issues head-on with practical advice for leaders that want to prepare the workforces of the future. Goldberg and Steven-Waiss challenge us to create new fluid approaches *and* provide a roadmap for doing so. For those looking for a new path forward, this is a must-read."

—Eva Sage-Gavin, senior managing director, head of Global Talent & Organization, Accenture

"A lack of career growth is now the number one reason why people leave their jobs. *The Inside Gig* shows business leaders how seamlessly artificial intelligence can match people to new and inspiring opportunities to grow their careers. Read it today to keep your employees engaged and inspired."

—Jeanne C. Meister, founding partner, Future Workplace,
and coauthor of *The Future Workplace Experience*

"This book is a definitive handbook for HR practitioners. Technology is enabling companies to do things that weren't easy otherwise. The emerging gig economy is changing the paradigms of talent and talent practices. A combination of these two aspects creates very exciting possibilities to build the future of the workplace."

—Aadesh Goyal, global chief human resources officer, Tata Communications

"*The Inside Gig* reinvents how to think about and deploy people inside an organization. By focusing on skills more than positions, companies flow talent to better solve problems and employees better fulfill their potential. The six principles, numerous cases and pragmatic tips make this a must-use book for anyone working to upgrade talent."

—Dave Ulrich, professor, University of Michigan, and partner, The RBL Group

"Goldberg and Steven-Waiss have delivered a compelling, innovative and actionable vision for the future of work. They have spent years collaborating with colleagues to figure out how to disrupt the 'business as usual' approach to managing talent to better align with the workplace that is defined by both technological empowerment and the democratization of work."

—John Boudreau, PhD, professor, Management & Organization,
University of Southern California

Edie Goldberg, PhD, and Kelley Steven-Waiss

The *Inside* Gig

How Sharing Untapped Talent Across Boundaries Unleashes Organizational Capacity

Cataloguing data available from Library and Archives Canada

ISBN 978-1-928055-60-0 (hardcover)
ISBN 978-1-928055-61-7 (EPUB)
ISBN 978-1-928055-67-9 (PDF)

Editor: Don Loney
Cover and interior design: Paul Dotey
Edie Goldberg's photo: Christophe Testi, CreativeShot Photography
Kelley Steven-Waiss's photo: Roel van Koppenhagen, No Point Studio

Published by LifeTree Media Ltd.
LifeTreeMedia.com

Distributed in the U.S. by Publishers Group West and in Canada by Publishers Group
Canada

Printed and bound in Canada

Dedication

We dedicate this book to our husbands, John and Vincent, who have let us pursue our passions, and to all employees who want to bring their full selves to work and to continuously learn and grow.

In Memoriam

To Christy Hamilton (Kelley's mom), a shining example of a woman in fearless pursuit of her passions and willingness to reimagine herself.

Table of Contents

FOREWORD

G oldberg and Steven-Waiss's book addresses an enormous and exis-
tential topic: the new world of work. We are all now "gig workers,"
even those of us with full-time jobs in large well-managed companies.

Let me explain. Over the last decade, digital tools and digital business
models have transformed businesses in every industry. Retailers are
digital sales and distribution companies; banks are digital commerce
and service companies; and workers in healthcare, pharmaceutical
companies, professional services and other industries are all now pow-
ered by digital tools.

The big change is not the tools or the technology: it's how they've
changed the *way* we work. In my latest study of talent trend (2019),
more than 35 percent of companies say they've shifted from hierarchy
to network as their primary organization model. Most of us now work
on projects and programs, our real job description is more of an estimate
of what we do. And in a company where our value is driven by our
contribution to the team, each of us have to make sure our skills and
teamwork capabilities are up to date.

I often call this the biggest disruption of all—rewiring a company
to operate in a digital way, not just build digital solutions.

In this world where we focus on work, not jobs, we are all in a sense gig workers now. Sometimes we carry on the responsibilities of our job description, but often we help others, contribute to a project, or lend our expertise to others. Internal talent mobility, an area of HR which was often neglected, is now one of the most important elements of talent management—forcing business and HR leaders to rethink what high potential really means.

And as far as leveraging external talent, this is an enormous new opportunity for companies. My latest study (2019) found that more than 35 percent of all workers operate in some gig fashion (full time or as a side hustle), yet only 12 percent of companies even know who their gig workers are. Companies often have 30–40 percent of their workforce on some contingent contract, but few have standards for hiring, management, development, and cultural integration of these people. This is all good stuff for HR to focus on, and this book will show you how.

Finally, this new world of highly interconnected teams, operating on projects around the world, demands a new type of leadership. The leaders of the future are often younger (40 percent of employees now work for someone younger than they are) and more interconnected, and they act more as a coach and enabler and less as a "boss." As gig workers, we are really responsible for our own successes and careers, so we need leaders who can facilitate and empower people in this kind of company.

As the book title describes, if you can learn how to leverage gig work for everyone, you can unleash untapped talent and drive organizational growth. This book will serve as a guide, and I think every business and HR leader should read it carefully.

Best wishes for the new world of work—the opportunities for all of us are endless!

Josh Bersin, global industry analyst
(www.joshbersin.com)

PREFACE

For us, this book was much more than a bucket-list item—it comes from an ambition to start a movement. We strongly believe that we have a vision of how to make work better and want to challenge the long-held paradigms about how work can and should be done. We believe this is good for employees, managers and the companies and shareholders they serve. We know the future of work is going to transform organizations. We believe that technology that is available today can enable an entirely new way of utilizing all the skills our employees bring to the company and create opportunities for continuous learning and growth.

We have deeply personal reasons for being so passionate about this topic, so we want to share our stories.

Kelley:

If someone had told me when I was a child that I would grow up some day and not only lead people, but change the world by building a technology platform that would revolutionize the way people work, I certainly would have said they were crazy. Despite having quite an active imagination, I don't believe I ever dreamed big enough and I often allowed other people to define me. As I look back on my life experiences and my story, I realize that everything that has happened to me personally and professionally is part of the fabric of who I am today—someone who is passionate about the future of work and the legacy that I hope to leave in my profession.

That journey to change the world really started in 1994 when my mother, Christy Hamilton, who had dreamed of becoming a police officer, finally got that chance to reimagine herself and change her career from an accountant to an officer for the Los Angeles Police Department (LAPD). She was 44 when the LAPD lifted the age ban for new cadets (prior to this time, women that age were not able to enter into law enforcement). She looked up to her father, a detective for the LAPD during her childhood, and now she would have an opportunity to follow in his footsteps, as she also dreamed about becoming a detective.

Despite what would be a grueling academy with physical challenges, especially for someone her age, she sailed through them with flying colors. In February 1994, she graduated at the top of her class and won an award for most inspirational cadet. Three days after graduating from the police academy, she was killed in the line of duty responding to a domestic violence dispute. Losing her so early caused a shockwave for the LAPD, but it also shocked the countless number of people who were inspired by her story and her ability to make good on a "second act" in her career.

It was a very difficult time for me, trying to make sense of this tragedy and all the questions about why this had to happen to her. However, in the emotional chaos, there was some peace in knowing that she'd had the opportunity to pursue a lifelong dream. It would later become one of the strongest and most meaningful messages that would define the rest of my life's work. My mother's experience taught me the importance of being able to reimagine yourself, pursue your passions, and be recognized as being able to contribute beyond what you are doing today based on the holistic portfolio of your experiences.

The tragedy surrounding her death became the catalyst for a dramatic change in my perspective about people and their professional journeys. It was the beginning of internalizing the "growth mindset"—the belief that people are not fixed beings; they have the ability to change and grow over time and are an amalgamation of all of their career and life experiences. This was a transformative realization and I wanted to find a way to bring the growth mindset to organizations and apply it.

As a human resources (HR) executive, I knew that the current HR systems had no way to operationalize this belief and solve for talent mobility at scale. Setting out to solve this problem, as my organization and others embarked on the future of work, became the genesis of the talent platform at HERE Technologies, and what would later become a commercialized solution in the market known as Hitch.

That life experience is a central reason for my strong belief in being able to pursue your passions and to reimagine yourself. I believe that everyone should be able to bring their whole selves to their work and that people are so much more than what they are doing today. And, much like my mother's example, I have had a "jungle gym" career. I have spent my career motivated to learn, grow and pursue my passions and interests. I have held so many roles and have had so many wonderful, diverse experiences that have shaped who I am today. My hope is that more people will adopt this new way of thinking—seeing themselves not as fixed beings but as full of opportunities to be reimagined several times throughout their career.

Edie:

It was early career experiences that created my awareness of how organizations box people in to a job and fail to recognize *all* of their skills. Before I started my own consulting firm nineteen years ago, I worked for Towers Perrin. While my role description was multi-faceted (Asia-Pac liaison for the Human Capital Management Practice; global thought leader in Career Management, Learning and Development, and Succession Planning), fundamentally I was a consultant in the Human Capital Consulting Practice. But my education and experience went far beyond the type of work we did within this practice area. I have a PhD in Industrial and Organizational Psychology, which included eight semesters of advanced statistical training and several courses in research methods. Earlier in my career, I had put this education into practice, and I was a deep expert in research methods.

A few years into my tenure with Towers Perrin, the company began to build a Measurement Practice, which was just forming in the west region. Despite my expertise, I was never allowed to participate in Measurement projects because I was not in that practice. Our organization was very siloed, and those barriers were rarely crossed. Lending my expertise to the Measurement Practice would have been a win-win. The firm would have more access to more expertise in the local market, and I would have gotten to do work that I think is, quite simply, fun.

The experience left a deep imprint on me as a talent management professional. Since that time, I have helped numerous companies (from Fortune 50 to smaller, privately held organizations) improve how they manage employee careers by helping them to deeply understand their own talent: people's passions, aspirations, past experiences, education and career interests. In my experience, companies can do a better job of understanding all the skills employees have and taking full advantage of the expertise each individual offers, even if it's not needed in their current role, and particularly during times of organizational transformations.

While Kelley points to her mom as a point of inspiration, I always love to hold up my husband, John Carter, as the ultimate example of a person with a portfolio career. Time and time again, he has understood what he is good at and where his passions lie, and then he has pivoted to doing something new that brings him energy. For example, based on his education in electrical engineering with an emphasis in acoustics, he began his career at Bose (he had studied under Amar Bose at MIT, so this is not a surprise). He quickly advanced in the ranks at Bose to become chief engineer, which gave him both general management skills and the financial acumen required to run a line of business.

With this experience, he pivoted to start a product development consulting firm. Once he realized that he had tired of the daily grind of consulting travel and he really loved managing a team, he sold his firm and became the CEO of a technology start-up. This experience helped him understand that what he really loved in this role was selling the technology the company developed to other companies. So he pivoted once again (and this was a *big* pivot) to become an investment banker, where he would help companies sell their company (and intellectual property assets) to other companies. After the 2008 downturn, he then decided to restart his product development consulting practice. This is a perfect example of an individual who has pivoted to entirely new careers to follow his interests and fully utilize all the skills he has. In the words of my dear friend Beverly Kaye, "Up is not the only way."[1] John's portfolio career represents the type of career growth opportunities we are trying to make available for more people.

It is with these experiences that we wish to bring the Inside Gig into action inside your organizations. We hope this book serves as both inspiration and opportunity to take action.

INTRODUCTION

Change can be frightening, and the temptation is often to resist it.
But change almost always provides opportunities—to learn new things,
to rethink tired processes, and to improve the way we work.
—Klaus Schwab

A NEW WAY OF OPERATING

A MYRIAD OF BOOKS DESCRIBE WHY, WHAT AND HOW work is being disrupted. Yet many companies are held captive by out-of-date tools, policies and practices that won't get them through this disruptive change. It is time to break the cycle.

We are passionate about helping organizations change in ways that will improve both organizational performance and employee experience. For four years, we worked with more than 70 chief human resource officers (CHROs) and HR thought leaders on the CHREATE Project: The Global Consortium to Reimagine HR, Employment Alternatives, Talent and the Enterprise.[1] Our collaboration over this time has informed our views about how the world of work is changing and how we need to alter the way we work in response. Specifically, we've realized that organization models need to evolve to be more responsive to the rapid shifts in skills, technology and business models. Our leadership roles in the CHREATE project gave us the opportunity to discuss these issues with forward-thinking HR leaders and test the ideas with business leaders of all types.

1

Since the CHREATE project, we have developed our own ideas about how to build a new talent operating model to help organizations apply the concept of the gig economy *inside* their firms. This model allows companies to share talent across boundaries by dynamically matching and deploying skills to work. We call it the Inside Gig. It creates competitive advantage through an employee experience that democratizes work, facilitates learning and unleashes internal capacity. We have put our ideas to the test within several organizations across different industries, and we have practical knowledge of how to make this change happen.

This book shares our ideas and experiences to help organizations understand how to move from traditional structures and ways of working into a new paradigm—one that better fits this rapidly shifting, dynamic business environment. It is also a playbook of ideas turned into actions to deploy a new talent operating model to address the needs and pace of work today and tomorrow. This playbook is based on six core principles that lay a foundation for operating in a new way, a way we believe will lead to increased productivity and greater levels of innovation.

THE INTERNAL NETWORK

In today's competitive landscape, companies need to develop fresh approaches to managing talent by leveraging new technologies and responding to changing business models that redefine employment relationships. It is no longer enough to have the most appealing employer brand, or the best university relations programs or even a best-in-class workspace, because it has become less clear how we define the *workforce*.

When new methods for competing for human resources via "talent on demand" gave rise to platforms such as Topcoder and Upwork, the idea of a workforce made up of both employees and temporary talent began to make a lot of sense. However, the rise of machine automation and the Internet of Things (IoT) has fundamentally transformed not only the nature of work but the speed at which it's necessary to learn and deploy new skills that are often in higher demand than supply. This remains true no matter how an organization plans to source talent. We must challenge what we thought was novel in talent management as recently as two to three years ago. Now it's a race to acquire *skills*. And just when everything seems under control, another emerging skill domain becomes both critical and scarce. Without a crystal ball, today's CEOs and CHROs are managing their most valuable competitive resource in the dark.

Enter a new era of competitive talent deployment via the internal gig network. Rather than acquire new skills by hiring from outside, the new and quite disruptive reality is that competitive advantage is now based on the ability to rapidly develop and better leverage the talent supply *within* a company. So, instead of focusing on competing for hot or in-demand skills that are in short supply and high demand, we suggest concentrating on what you have the power to control:

1. **Bring visibility to the internal skills** you have and any gaps there are (supply).
2. **Learn to accurately predict** what skills you might need (demand).
3. **Address the speed at which you can upskill** current talent for new or critical skill domains.
4. **Use digital horsepower**—through human-machine collaboration via predictive analytics, machine learning (ML), and automation—to accurately and efficiently match and deploy that talent to the right work, at the right time, at the right cost.

MORE THAN A JOB TITLE

It's often overlooked that before taking up their current positions, people had other roles, industry experiences, skills and interests. Most human capital management (HCM) systems categorize employees by job titles, not skills, though many systems link static job descriptions with requisite skills for those job titles. Even this simple organizing system is flawed because quite often employees can customize their job titles for niches they're in, thus making common jobs difficult to compare from a systems perspective. For example, a sales manager becomes a "fine wines sales manager," and a software developer becomes a "hacker" or "QuickBooks guru."

This difficulty aside, most employees are much more than their job titles. They bring past experiences and current passions that reflect different skills and abilities they can contribute to their organizations, even if those skills aren't applicable in their current role. For instance, to determine how many web designers a company might have, you would have to get beyond those individuals with "web designer" in their job titles. Some people are self-taught web designers and design websites as a hobby or for personal projects. To answer this question, you would need to survey the skills of these employees to know what talents they possess, regardless of the positions they have today.

Another common example is an employee, let's call her Kathy, who has a degree in engineering. Kathy's first job out of school was as a product marketing engineer. She realized she had a knack for understanding the importance of product features and benefits and communicating them to others. As a result, she followed a marketing path rather than an engineering one. However, at Kathy's core is her love of engineering; it was just that the opportunities in marketing at the time were interesting and challenging. She could have uniquely contributed to projects based on both her engineering and marketing expertise. But as her time with the company progressed, she remained a marketer, and no one considered asking her to participate in a project that required engineering abilities. Consequently, Kathy now feels that her skills are underutilized by her employer. She is more than her current job title and could offer far more to her employer if the organization thought of her as a whole person.

MAKING TALENT VISIBLE

If employees are more than their job titles, how do you improve the visibility of your company's talents and what can you do with this increased visibility? What can you learn from the gig economy and how can you apply some of that knowledge to your company? Most gig workers find their work on talent platforms (Upwork, Toptal, Guru, Fiverr, etc.) where those looking to hire an individual search a database of people who have specific skills for certain projects. The gig workers on the platform enter their skills and interests into the database. The talent platform then matches gig workers with opportunity providers. By mirroring such a system internally, organizations can gain greater visibility into their own talent.

In today's constantly changing business environment, organizations need to gain an in-depth understanding of the talent they have to both leverage the skills inside their companies and create strategies to transition employees to new kinds of work. Let's start with the first goal—better leveraging the talent you already have. Chapter 1 presents a new talent operating model; we expand on this model in Part Three: How to Make It Work. The new talent operating model is a way for organizations to identify and analyze talent based on skills, not job titles. This gives more insight into the complete set of capabilities within the organization beyond the bounds of job titles or résumés.

If Kathy's organization were to reduce its investment in marketing and shift more resources into innovation through its engineering team, her company could possibly avoid laying her off and she could pivot to an engineering role. Or a short-term project might arise that requires her engineering talent, when most of the existing engineering staff are overcommitted already. Kathy might enjoy a short-term, part-time project to use her engineering skills in addition to furthering the marketing expertise she gains in her current role.

Now let's address the need for strategies to transition employees to new kinds of work. Every day we're inundated with articles addressing the shifting business landscape and the quandary many organizations face of what to do with their current workforces when, because of technological advancements in the workplace, existing skills become obsolete and new skills are needed. When a company is undergoing significant strategic shifts, it is particularly important to gain greater insight into *all* of the skills in the company.

For example, in 2015 John Chambers, at the time CEO of Cisco

Systems, wrote about his company's shift from routers and switches to cloud computing and the IoT.[2] In February 2017, we interviewed Ian Bailie, who was then senior director, talent acquisition and people planning operations, at Cisco. He spoke about the importance of gaining visibility of the company's talent during its transition to the IoT. Bailie told us: "We needed to gain a better idea of the skills, knowledge and expertise of our employees. Cisco is going through a big transformation, and we are moving away from our core expertise. When we look at the external labor market, there are not enough of the skills we need to succeed in our move toward the Internet of Things. The idea of laying off people with the old skills and hiring people with the new skills we need is not really a viable option. We needed to minimize laying off talent by reskilling people for the future of work." Gaining visibility into the skills Cisco currently had gave the company insight into who might be able to make the transition to the newly required skill sets, and thus whom the company should focus on first for reskilling to grow the talent needed within the organization.

Cisco is a specific example of a company moving away from its core expertise to a new area of focus. But it is more and more common for organizations to experience shifting technologies, platforms and areas of attention based on evolving business needs and new strategic priorities. Many employees' future roles haven't been invented yet, an indication of how quickly the workplace is evolving. Companies can't assume they can lay off employees who possess an old set of skills and then hire employees with the necessary new skills. There are not enough people with those hot, in-demand skill sets available to satisfy all companies as they move to big-data analytics, virtual reality, artificial intelligence (AI) and so on.

Given this talent shortage, firms need to figure out how to build their own talent. Furthermore, reskilling the company's employees for the future of work is one tangible example of the Business Roundtable's redefinition of the purpose of a corporation, which expands the definition beyond serving only shareholders to also include serving customers, employees, suppliers and communities. Investing in employees and the communities a business serves is critical to its long-term success.

When skills become visible, any organization can then manage both its supply as well as the demand for such talent through requests on projects or open requisitions. Armed with this information, an organization can create talent strategies to close the supply-demand gap and prepare for future strategic shifts.

By gaining visibility into the hidden skills, capabilities and aspirations of their employees, organizations can more rapidly and cost-effectively match the right talent to solve real-time business challenges. They can also tap into discretionary effort from a highly engaged workforce by allowing employees to work on those projects that best match their skills and interests. The future is about connecting people with opportunities for micro-learning, personal growth and fully leveraging all of their capabilities so that they can lead more fulfilling careers and companies can maximize their investment in talent.

DIVERSITY AND CHOICE

It is often said that it is much easier to get a new job in a different company than it is to transfer to another department within the same organization. Employees today want new and different experiences. Yet most jobs are so specialized that people get stuck doing the same work over and over again, which leads to boredom and disengagement. Opportunities to work with different colleagues on different projects are exactly the type of dynamic learning experiences today's employees seek. When employees are exposed to new leaders, work with new team members or are able to use their skills in a different context, there are constant opportunities for learning and growth. Not only are new challenges presented in those work teams, but employees also learn from different leadership styles and from their coworkers' knowledge, skills and experiences.

Traditional job rotation programs have been around for a long time. Their main benefit is exposure to new managers, new teams and different types of work; they are a way of rapidly expanding an employee's set of experiences in a relatively brief time. To gain the same

7

amount of learning in a traditional role-based assignment would take many more years. Given that today's millennials demonstrate impatience with the speed of learning in a traditional job trajectory, some organizations have turned to job rotations to provide employees with new experiences. But with recently developed technological capabilities, there are new ways to provide diversity and choice in work rather than rely on traditional job rotation programs.

When Tata Communications, an Indian telecommunications company, surveyed its eight thousand employees, more than 50 percent said they were interested in changing their roles.[3] However, the organization's internal job rotation program could only handle about four hundred rotations per year. Tata Communications also found that most of its departments had a lot of programs and projects they needed to complete; however, they didn't necessarily have the skills on hand to get them done. This realization gave rise to the Tata Communications Project Marketplace, an internal opportunity platform. The company built its own system to capture the skills of current employees, then had managers post jobs in the marketplace that its employees could apply for.

Now, when employees finish projects in the marketplace, they get rated on their skills, much like the rating systems used by talent platforms such as Upwork, Fiverr and Wonolo. That way employees can shape their internal reputations around specific skills. Employees who take on projects do so on their own time, since they don't get released from any of their primary work responsibilities. Participation in the marketplace is strictly voluntary, and Tata Communications believes that only employees who can invest extra time in personal development choose to take part. The company also uses this program to familiarize managers with hiring for project-based work. The intention is to train managers through experience to consider what work should be a project and what work needs full-time dedicated employees.

As organizations build new people practices, they need to consider what the employee or manager expects from those practices. When it comes to what attracts new employees to a company, the research is very clear: career advancement opportunities, challenging work and opportunities to learn new skills.[4] So an ability to provide employees with a diverse set of experiences in which they can craft their own paths will likely attract the best talent. With the barriers to free-agent or contingent work being low and talent demanding more diverse work, greater choice and the opportunity to rapidly acquire new skills, there is pressure to create an employee experience like that of a free agent *inside* an organization.

By participating in short-term, part-time projects (much like a task-force committee assignment), employees get to learn while doing real and important work for their organizations. We are strong promoters of the idea that 70 percent of learning should come from on-the-job experiences. We just use the term *job* a little bit more loosely. When employees are allowed to opt in to projects where they can learn a new skill set, use a currently underutilized skill, or simply work in an area they're passionate about, they'll exert more discretionary effort because the work is based on their own personal interests.

THE CORE PRINCIPLES

In Part Three: How to Make It Work, we describe more fully this new talent operating model and the technology that enables the process. This new way of working is based on six core principles, which are elaborated on in Part Two; to be successful at implementing the new talent operating model, it is important to master each of them. These principles are briefly introduced here. At the end of each chapter in Part Two: The Core Principles, we've included a section called Perspectives from the Inside Gig that outlines how to put the principles into action from the perspective of the employee, manager or company.

Principle No. 1: You Get What You Give

Most members of the Generation X and baby boomer cohorts have grown up with a management style that focuses on owning and controlling employees on their teams or in their functions. For them, talent sharing across departments or functions is an uncomfortable concept. Allowing greater sharing of talent across organizational boundaries (*talent mobility*) can create abundance rather than scarcity of resources in an organization. Managers give away some of the time employees work to other departments; they can also get help from employees from different departments. Over time, this swapping of talent should equal out. The talent that managers are able to access this way might have a critical skill set not available from their current team members, but they don't need to bring in an external contractor or consultant or open a position requisition to hire a new employee for a skill that is not regularly needed. "You get what you give" is one of the most challenging mindset shifts necessary to embrace the new talent operating model.

Principle No. 2: Know What You Have

It's a common problem for companies not to be aware of the skills their employees bring to their organizations. At best, they know all of their employees' job titles. And companies don't take advantage of existing technology to monitor skill gaps and encourage employees to acquire new skills that are important to the company. Human capital management systems have traditionally been matched to an old infrastructure that emphasizes jobs and doesn't easily illustrate an inventory of skills. An ability to clearly identify the full range of skills within an organization allows talent acquisition and deployment to be optimized by focusing on filling strategic gaps for work that has to be performed today while planning effectively for skills that will be needed in the future.

The *talent supply chain* is an application of traditional inventory supply-chain management to talent. Supply-chain management is the optimization of product inventory and supplies so that those items can arrive on time and to the right destination. Similarly, a talent supply chain is based on skills inventories and knowing how much to have "in stock" to ensure that supply matches demand. Organizations that deploy those right skills at the right time will be well positioned when emerging skill domains (such as artificial intelligence) reach higher demand than supply. Failure to manage supply of skills efficiently could lead to loss of market share and profits, and ultimately, if a company doesn't have the skills that are crucial to pursue their strategic goals, failure to thrive.

Principle No. 3: Create a Learning Organization

Given that the half-life of skills is now only five years, employees must constantly update their learning. Millennials have a reputation for wanting continual career advancement. However, when we dig deeper to understand what that means, it is really a desire for nonstop learning and career growth. Being able to further their learning is an important incentive for employees in today's relentlessly evolving business environment because, without continuous learning, skills easily become irrelevant. However, organizations have a difficult time keeping up with employee demands for personalized, dynamic, ongoing learning and development opportunities, which require exposure to different experiences that build new skills. Gaining access to micro-learning opportunities facilitates skill acquisition and career growth more quickly than yesterday's approaches. Bite-size on-the-job learning and online learning have become the new normal for rapid skill development.

Principle No. 4: Democratize the Work

Millennials bring to the workforce a new set of values and expectations along with an inclination to be more entrepreneurial in nature and more in control of how, when and where they work. This drives a need for a more consumer-like experience, not unlike the ways employees experience their personal lives. They get to choose, for example, which airline to fly and when they want to go to fit their individual needs. When employees are allowed more freedom and choice in how they contribute in the workplace, they can select work that suits them. This flexibility helps employees get unstuck from narrowly defined roles and the boredom that comes with doing the same set of tasks day after day.

They are able to use the full breadth of skills they can contribute to their organizations. Using technology and artificial intelligence, companies can automatically match employees to potential opportunities, which opens up possibilities beyond the old boys' network, which only gives access to new projects to those who are politically connected within the company.

Principle No. 5: Create an Agile Organization

A move away from a traditional hierarchy toward more project-based teams can increase a company's responsiveness to changing business dynamics. Historically, organizations have been built to be efficient and effective, which was appropriate in a time of predictability. Organizational hierarchy was a natural outgrowth of this desire to be efficient. But the resulting business models created strong silos that discourage cross-boundary collaboration (e.g., sharing information across marketing and engineering). In today's era of unpredictability and constant business model disruption, organizations must be designed for speed, agility and adaptability to respond to evolving business priorities and customer demands. Part of designing for adaptability is a shift away from hierarchical structures toward models where work is accomplished in teams. Using self-managed work teams and providing appropriate support structures, the management and the workforce become more fluid and responsive to business needs while remaining focused on the goals the teams are designed to achieve.

Principle No. 6: Bust the Functional Silos

Breaking down organizational silos allows for cross-functional collaboration within the company to foster innovation. The resulting cross-pollination of ideas ensures that the product or service is representative of customers in a diverse marketplace. Individuals from different disciplines look at business challenges in different ways. When teams that represent a variety of disciplines focus on the same problem, diverse ideas can be generated and then combined to achieve novel solutions.

One of the greatest benefits of cross-functional collaboration is that employees are exposed to a different part of the business and thus gain greater insight into how the company operates as a whole.

A NEW TALENT OPERATING MODEL THAT LEVERAGES TECHNOLOGY TO IMPROVE AGILITY

Now is the time to disrupt the existing 20th-century operating models and create a new talent operating model that helps companies optimize their *internal* resources. With the advances made in artificial intelligence and machine learning, there are new and effective tools to deploy talent within organizations. But the technology only enables the process.

We believe the new talent operating model is the most critical component of the Inside Gig. It is about changing the way a company operates to best use and reskill the talent it currently has. To employ talent in a different and more dynamic way, modifications are needed in all areas of the talent operating model: culture, leadership, ways of working, HR programs and processes, team development processes and so on. However, you can't simply flip the switch and change to a new talent operating model overnight. Our approach lays out a 10-year road map detailing how an organization can build on smaller modifications to shift to the future of work.

Former U.S. president Barack Obama once said: "Change in the abstract is easy."[5] Truer words have seldom been spoken. In Part Four: The Inside Gig in Action, we lay out our recommendations for making a successful transition to a new talent operating model. We share case studies from two organizations—HERE Technologies and Tata Communications—that have made this transition, so you can learn from their experiences of successful implementations.

We believe the future of work will look very different than it does today. Organizations must adapt to become more agile as they shift and change based on new technologies, new skills and new business competitors. This book is a guide to one path to take in, as we like to say, "tiptoeing into the future of work." You can follow this path to create companies that are more productive and more innovative, while offering employee experiences that drive high levels of engagement and organizational performance.

PART ONE

The Time for the Inside Gig Has Come

In this volatile business of ours, we can ill afford to rest on our laurels,
even to pause in retrospect. Times and conditions change so rapidly
that we must keep our aim constantly focused on the future.
—Walt Disney

CHAPTER 1
Disrupting the Talent Operating Model

Once we rid ourselves of traditional thinking,
we can get on with creating the future.
—James Bertrand

WHAT IS A TALENT OPERATING MODEL DESIGNED TO DO?

H OW OFTEN DO YOU THINK OF THE OPERATING model your company is built on? You might think about your car's operating system more than you do about how work flows and gets done—especially when the "check engine" light comes on. Let's begin by discussing current operating models and then open the door to our ideas about what change is possible and even imminent in the way work is done.

Organizations are built on operating models and systems designed to deliver value to their customers and shareholders. An operating model links strategy, organization design and execution. While many operating model designs can be found in various books and articles, for our purposes we have adopted the one shown in Figure 1.1 Operating Model.

Figure 1.1 Operating Model

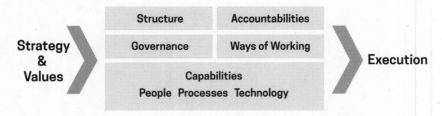

Marcia Blenko, Eric Garton and Ludovico Mottura, "Winning Operating Models That Convert Strategy to Results," Bain & Company, December 10, 2014, www.bain.com/insights/winning-operating-models-that-convert-strategy-to-results.

In this model, *strategy and values* are defined by an organization's leadership team; they provide the foundation upon which a company operates. The first three areas of the operating model—structure, accountabilities and governance—are owned by the executive leadership team. *Structure* refers to the high-level organization chart that sets out how a company organizes itself to take advantage of scale and expertise. It provides an understanding of how resources are organized and coordinated—functional lines of business versus matrixed structures; global centers of operation or distributed authority to regions. *Accountabilities* delineate the roles and responsibilities for the organization's primary entities, including where accountability for performance (profit-and-loss ownership) lies. *Governance* refers to how processes and activities that cut across structures are managed or regulated, particularly as related to information flow and decision-making. It describes the management processes or operating committees that participate in making decisions on business priorities, including how resources are allocated and how organizational performance is measured and managed.

The *ways of working* address four people-related processes:

1. Organization culture
2. Leadership behaviors that support the business strategy
3. Decision-making styles and processes
4. Organization design to optimize performance across the company

Finally, the *capabilities* of a company (people, processes and technology) focus on areas that are also usually within the realm of HR, but not exclusively. Capabilities involve defining the type of talent or resources that are needed and how to focus their efforts; the processes that specify how a company attracts, manages and rewards its employees; and the technology that's adopted to ensure organizational productivity.

Figure 1.1 Operating Model is a visual representation of how an organization operates. In this book, when we refer to a *talent operating model*, we are focusing on the ways of working and the capabilities that an organization cultivates to execute its strategy and goals. This chapter offers a broad description of the talent operating model that underpins a new way of working—the Inside Gig—and how this model differs from traditional talent operating models.

TYPES OF TALENT OPERATING MODELS

Traditional Talent Operating Models

Traditional talent operating models generally define the ways of working and capabilities that support the organization in achieving its goals. While aspects of culture and leadership behaviors are unique to each company, most organizations have decision-making styles and an organization design that support a hierarchical management style. Command-and-control systems are the epitome of traditional talent operating models; however, some organizations, while still hierarchical, have adopted collaborative approaches to work. In these organizations, decision-making styles and organization design might encourage collaboration, but important decisions are still made at the top. The capabilities these companies develop mirror this relatively stable work ecosystem.

In a traditional talent operating model, candidates interview for a specific job because they have a defined set of skills that meet the requirements for that role. Candidates are provided with a job description

gationTHE INSIDE GIG

that details the day-to-day responsibilities of the role and the skills needed to be successful in it. This specificity helps the organization hire the right person for the right role. The traditional model assumes that jobs are well defined, and while employees with similar positions have similar job descriptions, this model defines the unique set of tasks each role serves in the company.

Employees are expected to work on tasks or projects that require the skill set for which they were hired. The traditional model generally ignores other skills the candidate or employee might have that are irrelevant to the job at hand. Employees are supervised by a manager in their function (e.g., finance, HR, legal, engineering) and most if not all of their direction comes from within their function. Employees' upward mobility is generally perceived to be within their specific team or, possibly, function. Typically, career progression is viewed as a promotion up a career ladder.

Standard progression is up a career ladder within a certain sub-function is because it is often difficult for an employee to transfer across sub-functions (e.g., moving within the finance department from financial planning and analysis to tax or treasury; or in HR, from benefits to compensation), unless they are directly supported by a manager who pushes for this type of move. Part of the reason employees get so tied to their sub-specialties is a narrow task focus within the organization. Work is typically performed within the silo in which the employee executes their day-to-day responsibilities. While many employees would argue that their job descriptions quickly become outdated and that they're asked to do tasks outside their job descriptions, they nevertheless remain stuck and are forced to rely on the skills or capabilities for which they were hired. Over time, employees often find this tiresome and they become a flight risk.

Innovation-Focused Talent Operating Models

Some companies that are more innovation-focused have adopted a slightly different talent operating model. We'll call it an innovation-focused talent operating model. In this model, employees spend 80 percent or more of their time performing the responsibilities outlined in their job descriptions, and they may devote 15 percent to 20 percent of their time to work on innovation projects of their choosing. Employees may define their own innovation projects and recruit others to participate, or they may take part in projects started by others. While 3M has been operating under this model successfully since its inception in 1902 (Post-it Notes were invented using "15 percent time"), Google popularized the notion of "20 percent time." Whether it's 15 percent or 20 percent time, it's all about giving employees permission to work on a passion project that may have nothing to do with current business goals or objectives. According to 3M's Karen B. Paul, "Fifteen percent time is not a timesheet issue or corporate policy, it's a philosophy. It could be 5 percent of someone's time or it could be closer to 100 percent for some special projects. The idea is about giving employees space to work on projects they are passionate about."[1]

Anecdotally, we have learned from several sources that rather than their jobs being 80 percent core job responsibilities and 20 percent innovation time, their positions are 120 percent. Time allocated to working on innovation projects is added onto a 100 percent time commitment to their "real" jobs. But their additional innovation time gives them permission to work on projects of their own choosing with a self-selected group of people. This isn't part of working on the regular business needs of the company—serving customers, addressing pressing product issues—it's about discovering or inventing something new that isn't currently a product or service offered by the company.

For these organizations, the culture and leadership behaviors support the notion that allowing employees to have time to work on projects of their own choosing serves the company well. For example, Laszlo Bock, in his book *Work Rules!*, shares a core tenet of the Google culture: "If you give people freedom, they will amaze you."[2] Similarly, William McKnight, the president (1929–49) and chairman (1949–69) of 3M, said: "If you put fences around people, you get sheep. Give the people the room they need."[3]

These organizations have structures and decision-making processes that support innovation work and define how innovation projects get presented to governing bodies to turn them into company-funded projects. While most of the capabilities for these organizations roughly mirror a traditional talent operating model, their reward structures provide incentives to individuals who make important discoveries or create valuable new products for their companies.

So, in companies that use an innovation-focused talent operating model, while employees get some choice and diversity in the projects they work on because they can opt in to special ventures, they're still responsible for accomplishing the day-to-day responsibilities for the roles they were hired to do. The organization plays no role in directing people to work on projects based on their knowledge, skills, abilities or past work experiences. Employees are able to choose projects to work on.

Career progression in the innovation-focused talent operating model may be more fluid than in the traditional model, because of relationships formed while working on innovation projects. However, it remains a challenge to find opportunities outside a team or department, which usually inhibits these types of moves as an organizational norm.

Inside Gig Talent Operating Models

The operating model for the Inside Gig is different from both traditional and innovation-based talent operating models. The Inside Gig model is based on the premise that the time allocated to work on projects outside the regular scope of an employee's day-to-day job is (a) integrated into the employee's regular workweek and not specifically identified as innovation time or added on to an already challenging work schedule; and (b) centered on the mission-critical work that the company has to do. It is our fundamental belief that employees have far more capability than their workplace acknowledges and uses, when it comes to solving current business challenges. For example, developing products defined in an organization's current product development road map, resolving a customer service problem, or improving a current process that isn't performing to expectations. This is what the Inside Gig model is all about; it's not about investing an employee's resources in blue-sky activities.

However, a positive side-effect of the Inside Gig model is that it can spark innovation. This is an important benefit for any manager to understand. Innovation is a direct consequence of people working together from different parts of a business (e.g., marketing, sales and engineering), each of whom may bring a different perspective to the project. It also helps to generate more empathy and understanding of how work is accomplished in different parts of the business, because people share what they need to do to achieve the team's goals. Naturally, the more sharing and relationship building that occurs, the greater the likelihood that new ideas will emerge.

The Inside Gig talent operating model leverages the talent a company has to solve current business challenges. It gives employees opportunities to contribute skills they don't use in their day-to-day jobs and gain new skills while getting real work done.

You would be right to think that sharing talent across organizational boundaries requires managers and their team members to negotiate what aspects of team members' current roles can be automated, outsourced or given up completely because they're not value-added. Alternatively, there may well be aspects of a specific role that could be outsourced or assigned to someone else in order to allow an employee to learn something new or use a skill that is underutilized in their current position. This makes room for a portion of the employee's time to be allocated to work on projects outside their current job description. It could be 15 percent or 20 percent of the employee's time on an ongoing basis, or up to 100 percent of an employee's time for a short duration. With this time, employees can choose to volunteer for projects that let them utilize skills they have but are not putting to use in their current job. They can also learn new skills that will make them more valuable to the company, or simply work on projects that are aligned with their passions or interests.

The matching of skills and interests to opportunities is accomplished using artificial intelligence; in other words, through computers that find the best match of employee skills to the skills needed for specific projects. This gives employees equal access to new experiences in different parts of the business that they previously had no means of finding out about. It also supports diversity and inclusion by eliminating inadvertent human bias as employees seek access to new opportunities to enhance their skills.

Working on cross-functional projects enables employees to construct broader networks within the company to facilitate internal moves that align with their career aspirations. It also increases employees' understanding of the business, not just what happens within their teams. Career progression in the Inside Gig model offers a mosaic of experiences that advances employees via exposure to different opportunities that build breadth and depth, making them increasingly valuable to the organization and more marketable to other companies. We'll go into the specifics in more detail in Part Three: How to Make It Work.

KEY TAKEAWAYS

- Traditional talent operating models are designed so that organizations can hire individuals to fill prescribed roles that fit their knowledge, skills and experiences. Employees are expected to devote 100 percent of their time to deliver on the tasks and responsibilities of their jobs.

- Innovation-focused talent operating models provide employees with implicit permission to devote some of their time at work (generally 15 percent to 20 percent) to projects that suit their personal interests and passions. While these projects need to advance the business in some manner, they're not related to any current ongoing venture the company is dedicated to pursuing. Because employees are still responsible for getting their day-to-day jobs done, this often equates to 120 percent time.

- The Inside Gig talent operating model differs from innovation-focused talent operating models in that the percentage of time individuals take away from their day-to-day responsibilities is used to positively contribute to ongoing business projects. Employees work with their managers to reallocate tasks and responsibilities to make room for different work, which lets them leverage skills and abilities they have but don't use in their day-to-day jobs, work in areas they want to learn and grow in professionally, or simply explore work they're deeply interested in doing. The use of technology to match skills and interests to opportunities gives employees equal-opportunity access to projects.

REFLECTION POINTS

What problems are you and your team trying to solve that are proving difficult and could benefit from alternative perspectives?

Do people outside your department come to mind that you would like to bring to the table?

Is there any flexibility built into your company's talent operating model that can stretch people's skills to facilitate learning and make new connections? If not, do you think there is an opportunity for a trial venture?

CHAPTER 2
The Fourth Industrial Revolution and Its Impact on Business

A new type of thinking is essential if mankind is to survive
and move toward higher levels.
—Albert Einstein

THE FORCES SHAPING THE WORLD OF WORK

WHETHER YOU ARE A TEAM MEMBER or you lead a team, large or small, you will have noticed that the world of work is changing, a consequence of the way the world in general is changing. For one thing, countries like the United States and Canada are experiencing higher levels of racial and ethnic diversity through international immigration patterns. According to the Pew Research Center, by 2055, the United States won't have a single racial or ethnic majority.[1] This shift in demographics is naturally affecting the workforce, which is becoming more diverse by gender, culture, religion, sexual preferences and identification. The burning question facing organizations is how their talent operating model is set up to accommodate the diversity of thought, personal and professional experience, and work habits that people bring to the workplace every day.

Most notably, the workforce is simultaneously growing older (because baby boomers aren't retiring) and younger, with the rise of the millennial generation. Millennials currently make up more than half of the workforce and bring with them high expectations for work experiences that provide them with purpose and meaning at work. They want continuous learning and development opportunities that will result in rapid career progression.

Gallup has studied millennials for several years. In its 2016 report, *How Millennials Want to Work and Live*, it challenged the notion that they're a generation of job hoppers, a bad reputation that has been unfairly pinned on them. Research by Gallup indicates that 55 percent of millennials are simply not engaged at work. Many don't want to job-hop, but their companies fail to give them compelling reasons to stay. This is a product of the traditional talent operating model that boxes people in with a culture that roadblocks learning, growth and taking on new challenges. In today's tight talent markets, every organization needs to constantly provide employees with significant motivation to stay.[2]

Maynard Webb and Carlye Adler, the authors of *Rebooting Work*, provide a framework that illustrates how work is changing and what organizations have to do to engage their employees. They write about the millennials' high levels of disengagement and their need to embrace their entrepreneurial spirit and take control of their careers by seeking fulfilling work. Webb and Adler contrast four philosophies of work (see Figure 2.1). They believe that whether you start your own company or work for another person, you can be the "CEO of Your Own Destiny" and embark on a path to a gratifying career.[3]

Webb and Adler further argue that the rise in freelance work might have been prompted by the economic downturn and people looking for employment, but it has nevertheless inspired a generation to take more control over their careers, reduce commuting time and leverage technology to work anywhere at any time. This concept fits well with their desire to integrate work and life and to be more in command of their work options.

Technology and Obsolescence

Early signs of the unprecedented velocity, scope and impact of what has been called the Fourth Industrial Revolution are becoming apparent. Previous industrial revolutions made substantial improvements in the way we farmed; brought us into the Industrial Age, ushered in mass

Figure 2.1 Four Philosophies of Work

	Paternalistic Era	Age of Entrepeneurship
Meritocracy: Feels personally invested, proactive, positive, willing	**The Company Man/Woman** • High achiever • Great attitude • On the promotion track • In it for life	**CEO of Your Own Destiny** • Highly successful • Self-aware • Loving the freedom this choice has given you • Opt-in to being fully on the team every day • Build a network outside of the company "walls" • Have great and fulfilling career options
Entitlement: Feels deserving, frustrated, critical	**Disenchanted Employee** • Waiting to be discovered or recognized for your personal talents • Can't understand why others don't recognize how good you are • Not progressing in your career at the speed you expected • Believe your circumstances are someone else's problem	**Aspiring Entrepreneur** • Fully embracing control of your own destiny • Do not have enough work to do under the terms you are willing to do it • May not be addressing the gaps between your desires and your skills

Maynard Webb and Carlye Adler, *Rebooting Work: Transform How You Work in the Age of Entrepreneurship* (San Francisco: Jossey-Bass, 2013).

production; and eventually propelled us into the Information Age, whose eruption of technology and available information makes it easier to access facts and find talent through the Internet with job boards like Monster and social networks like LinkedIn.

Klaus Schwab from the World Economic Forum defines the Fourth Industrial Revolution as one characterized by a range of new technologies fusing the physical, digital and biological worlds, impacting all disciplines, economies and industries, and even challenging ideas about what it means to be human.[4] According to the World Economic Forum, four specific technological advances are significantly disrupting the world of work: high-speed mobile Internet, widespread adoption of big-data analytics, artificial intelligence and cloud technology.[5]

These new technologies are economic game changers, and the rate of change for new technologies remains unabated. So does disruption in all sectors, from retail to health care. With respect to people, the capital investments an organization is making in new technologies have short- and long-term implications. People need to be trained, and often in a hurry. But can a talent operating model—perhaps even yours— that is designed for a different time keep up?

Here is a prime example of technological advances creating disruptions. In 2001, people who lived in Oakland, California, and worked in San Francisco had to drive an hour in traffic, pay a $3 toll to cross a bridge, and spend $40 a day to park their cars. Many of these people lived too far away from public transit to make it convenient to get to work. But then an interesting change occurred. "Casual carpool," a new social phenomenon that hundreds of thousands of commuters used to travel to work, sprung up all over the East Bay. Every morning, people lined up at predetermined spots (generally bus stops) and waited for drivers to come by to pick them up to form carpools. The drivers then proceeded over the Bay Bridge and dropped their passengers off in downtown San Francisco. As an added bonus, carpools were allowed to cross the bridge for free and had access to expedited lanes. Never did these carpoolers imagine that less than a decade later, mobile technology and big data would be leveraged to create Uber, a ride-share service similar to casual carpooling, but now, of course, not free. This is just one way technology has disrupted our world—in this case causing a massive panic in the taxi industry by launching a system where people are more in control of their transportation experiences.

The Half-Life of Skills

In 2011, Douglas Thomas and John Seely Brown stated that the half-life of the skills we learn is only five years. New technologies or transformations in business practices will make half of what we know obsolete in a five-year span.[6] With the amount of change we've experienced in the past decade, the half-life of skills is even shorter today. According to the World Economic Forum, by 2022, the core skills required to do a job will shift by 42 percent, resulting in the loss of an estimated 75 million jobs.[7] However, media drama about robots taking over jobs is a slight exaggeration. Although many jobs will be lost to automation, several sources also estimate a net gain of new jobs due to digital transformation.[8] The World Economic Forum predicts this increase will amount to 133 million new jobs, a net gain of 58 million.[9]

By 2020, 14 percent of the global workforce may need to switch occupations due to digitization, artificial intelligence and automation.[10] As a result of the Fourth Industrial Revolution, an unparalleled shift in the skills required by the workforce is occurring. The hot jobs today—full-stack developers, user experience designers, cloud developers, data analysts and AI engineers—didn't even exist a decade ago, so who knows what the next hot skill set will be.

In their book, A New Culture of Learning, *authors Douglas Thomas and John Seely Brown tell us that "the half-life of a learned skill is 5-years," meaning that half of what we know will become obsolete in that time because of new technology or transformations in business practices.*

This new world of work has enormous potential to fulfill the desire of millennials to find more purpose and meaning in work. As the more mundane aspects of their jobs are removed, they are able to contribute to the success of their companies in completely different ways. Aaron Hurst's book *The Purpose Economy* shares how millennials want to build opportunities for self-expression into their day-to-day roles. But that, of course, requires new skills.[11]

Fifty-three percent of U.S. CEOs think their companies should retrain workers when jobs are eliminated through automation.[12] Unfortunately, only the highest-skilled workers receive reskilling, if it happens at all.[13] With the rapid pace at which skills are changing, companies must develop new strategies to upskill and reskill within the flow of work. It is not practical to expect employees to devote time to leave the workforce or take time away from their jobs to keep up with the skills necessary to compete today. However, if organizations don't find new approaches to revamp their talent operating model, the world of work will move from one that can provide employees with meaningful work to one that increases the gap between the haves and have-nots.

But not all the responsibility should reside with organizations. Employees must proactively pursue continuous learning opportunities to ensure their skills don't become obsolete. Governments must provide incentives and facilitate the creation of public-private partnerships to encourage companies to invest in reskilling their employees.

As we advance further into the Fourth Industrial Revolution, it is imperative for companies to rethink the way they work. The speed of change continues to accelerate. The need to adapt and pivot is becoming critical for everyone.

The Rise and Makeup of Adaptive Teams

According to Deloitte's *Global Human Capital Trends 2016*,[14] in the face of the forces that are reshaping the world of work, companies understand the urgency of doing away with traditional, hierarchical and functional models. These models will be replaced with flexible teams that are more agile and customer-focused, and better connected and integrated across functional lines.

Organizations have historically been built to be efficient and effective, which was appropriate in an era of predictability. The resulting business models established strong silos that discouraged cross-boundary collaboration. But in today's era of unpredictability and constant business model disruption, companies must be designed for speed and agility to allow them to respond better to business priorities and customer demands. As a result, organizations are creating flatter, more fluid structures.

Imagine work teams coming together to find solutions to business challenges or to innovate new products. These teams would assemble to achieve their objectives, and when they finished, disband and move on to different projects. While some organizations already operate in this manner, parallels are often drawn to the way work gets accomplished in Hollywood. A director pulls together a multi-disciplinary team that includes actors, scriptwriters, camera operators, makeup artists, visual effects people, costume designers and so on. When the film is completed, these talented and skilled people move on to other projects.

Today's business challenges are often too complex for one discipline within the organization to develop a solution or devise a fresh approach. To look at problems from different perspectives and arrive at optimal solutions, it helps to bring together diverse teams. This deliberate team structure is often seen in the biotech industry, where new product development teams are put together. To advance a molecule to a drug that will be a viable product, it takes the expertise of many disciplines to understand all the complexities. The shift to team-based work structures enables companies to be more agile because of the impermanence of these groups. These groups can be quickly formed, expanded, reduced or eliminated based on changing business dynamics. According to a 2019 Mercer report, the highest return on investment on talent will come from redesigning jobs to better deliver value.[15]

Delivering better value to a large part will depend on the leader's ability to align and optimize the talent and skill of team members who represent multiple generations, and so have different needs and approaches to problem solving based on their personal experiences. For example, baby boomers grew up with a mindset of "hard work pays off for an individual, and individual accomplishments matter." Conversely, millennial employees were taught from an early age to work in teams to solve problems, were rewarded for their "collective success," and have seldom encountered individual awards.

Millennials' inclination to collaborate has been of great benefit to them. They are entering an era of work that has grown increasingly complex and requires the input of people from different disciplines with different skills. Don't underestimate this change in the nature of work. A study published in the *Harvard Business Review* (**HBR**) reports that the growing complexity of work means that the time spent by managers and employees in collaborative activities has ballooned by 50 percent or more over the past two decades.[16]

So, for multiple generations, employee experiences that suit very different work styles and cultural backgrounds must be balanced with significant shifts in how work is accomplished. All of this is an out-growth of the burgeoning complexity of work and the need to connect across boundaries in organizations in ways that were never done before. Outmoded talent operating models will not be up to the challenge.

THE NEED FOR DIVERSITY AND CHOICE:
A CONSUMER EXPERIENCE

Looking at the five most prevalent forces driving change in the workplace (see Figure 2.2 Five Forces of Change), two themes illustrate why you need to offer employees greater choice in personal work experiences—democratization of work, and technological empowerment. The five forces of change are as follows:

- **Social and organizational reconfiguration:** Increased democratization of work creates a shift away from hierarchy in favor of more power-balanced organizations and communities that are less employment-based and more project-based. Talent will increasingly "join" based on aligned purpose.

- **All-inclusive global talent market:** Work is seamlessly distributed around the globe with 24/7 operations enabled by new corporate and social policies. Extreme longevity allows mature talent to stay in the workforce longer, while women and nonwhite ethnicities become talent-market majorities.

- **A truly connected world:** The world is progressively connected through mobile devices that allow work to be done from anywhere by a network of freelancers. New media enable global and real-time communications to speed up ideation, product development and go-to-market strategies.

- **Exponential pattern of technology change:** Technological breakthroughs increasingly disrupt markets and businesses. The rapid adoption of robots, autonomous vehicles, commoditized sensors, artificial intelligence and global collaboration will renew the rethinking of work.

• **Human-machine collaboration:** Advances in analytics, algorithms and automation continue to make improvements in productivity and decision-making. Smarter computing increasingly automates and abolishes mundane tasks previously performed by humans.[17]

Figure 2.2 Five Forces of Change

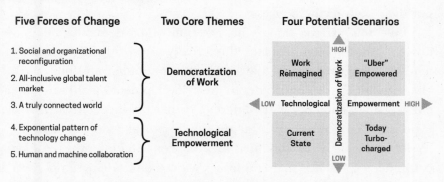

CHREATE, 2018, http://chreate.wpengine.com/2018/02/15/tools/.://chreate.wpengine.com/2018/02/15/tools/.

The first three forces of change speak to the theme of *democratization of work*, where a new vision of the future is characterized by new "employment" relationships that are shorter in duration and place into balance the needs of the individual and the needs of the company. A shift toward a more agile and responsive view of work will deliver results by activating purpose-built networks such as teams that work on common goals.

The last two forces speak to *technological empowerment*, where technology is transforming the way we live and work. Machine learning, 3D printing, mobile, wearables and algorithmic analytics are some of the many technologies that promise to empower individuals. New technologies allow people to work from anywhere at any time, and, within the scope of privacy laws and company regulations, provide greater insights into the workforce.

These forces of change in the workplace make it obvious that companies must dispense with talent operating models where the power in employment relationships is centralized and employees are boxed into narrowly prescribed roles. Given the proliferation of on-demand talent platforms—such as Topcoder, Toptal, Figure Eight, InnoCentive, Upwork, and Guru—there is no longer a necessity to create a "job" for every need an organization has at the moment. Because a significant amount of work can be broken down into discrete tasks or projects, companies can access the specific skills required now and let the individuals involved then move on to other projects where they can put their skills to the best use.

While this can be done with external or on-demand talent, the process can also be implemented internally to provide employees with new, challenging projects that keep them interested and engaged. It also simultaneously contributes to their development by offering different work assignments with different people in the company, while exposing them to new skills of growing importance to the firm. This choice to decide what work fuels their passions and interests is the new consumer experience that employees want today. Giving employees a technological solution that makes choosing work assignments as easy as ordering from Amazon brings the dynamic of today's consumer experience into the workplace.

The New Employment Contract: Continuous Learning

Before we address the research supporting an employee's desire to learn and grow, let's consider the issue from a company's perspective. Skills, not jobs, will become the new currency of the labor market.[18] We've already seen that in today's rapidly changing business environment the half-life of skills is less than five years. This means we all have to embrace a lifetime of learning rather than continue with the old mindset where we spend the first part of our lives learning, the next phase working and the last stage in retirement. Such a transformation is particularly needed because we are living longer and are likely to experience several different careers in the course of a lifetime.

A study by McKinsey & Company in late 2017 found that 66 percent of top executives said retraining and upskilling their employees were urgent business priorities.[19] More than 8 out of 10 global managers view learning as an important or very important issue for organizations today.[20] However, companies are aware that they aren't keeping up with the demand for personalized, dynamic, continuous learning opportunities. As a result, they're shifting to self-directed practices that enable people to develop themselves: on-the-job learning, access to massive online open courses (MOOCs) or other online content curated for their experiences. Cementing the importance of continuous learning for organizations, recent Glassdoor data reveal that the "ability to learn and progress" is now the key driver of a company's employment brand.[21] So, in today's highly competitive talent market, continuous learning is a business priority. Furthermore, LinkedIn's 2018 *Workforce Learning Report* indicates 93 percent of employees would stay at a company longer if the company invested in their careers.[22]

Studies of the attitudes of new college graduates in the United States and United Kingdom found some alarming results.[23] When new college graduates enter the workforce, they report being eager, prepared, passionate and committed, but one or two years later, those same graduates feel disillusioned, underemployed and undervalued. These individuals are looking for a more personalized experience at work, where their passions will be acknowledged and their career paths or work experiences are customized to their interests.

By creating an Inside Gig experience, companies can offer employees a better learning experience, improved variety in career development, and the possibility of keeping them engaged in corporate strategy, all of which will help them utilize their skills and not feel underemployed. According to a 2019 Mercer report, 51 percent of employees are willing to take an internal gig to gain experience, up from 38 percent in 2018.[24]

Through a series of interviews with companies experimenting with project-based opportunity platforms, we have learned that innovative companies are trying to help employees identify prospects for real-time learning. While almost all of these organizations provided these learning experiences on top of employees' regular work responsibilities, the opportunities offered employees the ability to leverage skill sets in new contexts or grow skill sets by applying them in a larger or different manner than they were able to do in the past. Connecting employees to the learning possibilities they desire is perceived to be highly valuable to both employees and employers. Learning has become an important commodity for employees in a constantly evolving business environment where skills can quickly become obsolete if learning isn't continuous.

The New Employment Contract: Meeting Changing Expectations

As organizations build people practices, they need to consider what employees or managers want or expect. To attract new employees to a company, the research is clear: career advancement, challenging work and opportunities to learn new skills are essential.[25] So providing employees with a diverse set of experiences in which they can craft their own path will help organizations entice the best talent in the marketplace.

Most companies that have experimented with internal talent networks have done so for the same reason—they're trying to retain their best talent. It is often said that it is much easier to get a job in a different company than it is to transfer to a different department within the same firm. Employees today want new and different experiences. Yet most jobs are so specialized that people get "stuck" doing the same work over and over again, which leads to boredom and disengagement. If employees don't get the work experiences they want, they won't hesitate to leave in search of better opportunities. A chance to work with different people on different projects is exactly the type of dynamic learning experience today's employees seek.

So what can we learn from the gig economy? While flexibility and control are the chief reasons people freelance, the ability to choose projects is also important to them, especially for full-time freelancers. Furthermore, freelancers are 24 percent more likely to feel their work gives them the opportunity to pursue projects they're passionate about or find meaningful, and they're 14 percent more likely to feel their work provides them with opportunities for learning and growth.[26]

So two significant reasons for the increase in gig work in companies are freelancers' desire to select what work they engage with, and the need for companies to acquire greater agility in terms of capacity and capability. With the barriers to free-agent or contingent work being low, talent demanding more diverse work and greater choice, and the opportunity for rapid acquisition of new skills, there is pressure to create an employee experience and mindset like that of a free agent *inside* organizations.

This is the question for companies to consider: Can you provide people with the experiences they want *inside* the organization rather than have them rely on freelancing to achieve greater diversity and choice in their work? We believe the answer is *yes*! The six core principles presented in Part Two create a foundation to attract the best talent, improve organizational productivity, foster innovation and enable companies to be more agile and stay ahead of the competition.

KEY TAKEAWAYS

- The global workforce is more diverse than ever before in terms of gender, age, culture, religion, sexual preference and identification. Creating a one-size-fits-all employee experience no longer works.

- The Fourth Industrial Revolution has created technological advances that have disrupted industries and the way we work, resulting in massive shifts in the skills needed in the workplace. Job losses due to skill obsolescence, though significant, will be surpassed by the growth of new jobs that never existed before, requiring new skills that aren't widely available in the labor market.

- Organizations need to be more agile and responsive to the changes created by the Fourth Industrial Revolution. Organizational hierarchy and functional silos are being replaced by flatter, more fluid structures that rely on purpose-built networks of teams.

- The democratization of work puts more control in the hands of em-ployees. These employees want more choice and diversity in the projects they work on so that they can continuously learn and fully utilize all of the skills they have to contribute to the success of their company.

- By creating an Inside Gig experience, a more agile work environment can leverage the full set of capabilities within an organization and unleash capacity by helping employees tap into their passions and fuel a continuous learning opportunity. This allows a company to build the skills needed as new technologies emerge in the workplace.

REFLECTION POINTS

How are the demographics of your company changing?

Has this change in demographics resulted in a shift in employee expectations? If so, how would you describe your employees' expectations?

How rapidly are skills changing within your company (as a whole or in parts of the business)?

Are you experiencing a greater need for cross-boundary collaboration to solve business problems? How easily are you able to form cross-disciplinary teams?

PART TWO
The Core Principles

The man who grasps the principles can successfully
select his own methods. The man who tries methods,
ignoring principles, is sure to have trouble.
—Harrington Emerson

CHAPTER 3
Principle No. 1: You Get What You Give

I have learned that the best way to lift one's self up is to help someone else.
—Booker T. Washington

IMAGINE A CUSTOMER SERVICE team meeting. You've convened to solve a problem that has a direct bearing on the customer experience. It's not that you haven't tried before, but the fixes haven't been working and customer complaints have not decreased. You are happy to see Lucinda enter the room and be warmly greeted by the team. Lucinda is from HR and has worked tirelessly on the employee experience. You ask a team member to outline the problem and the fixes you've tried to date. Can Lucinda shed any light on the challenge? She asks for 24 hours and to reconvene the team the next day.

At the next meeting, Lucinda offers some suggestions based on her work. Her perspective points to a communication issue that can be addressed by having a five-minute team huddle at the beginning and end of each work day to address issues that are affecting customers. You call Lucinda's manager to thank her for Lucinda's time.

The first Inside Gig principle, "You get what you give," addresses the importance of creating a give-and-get model around talent, specifically how sharing talent across departments or functions optimizes organizational resources. This principle suggests that a manager should *give* employees time to participate in projects outside their teams, either to use skills they have but aren't utilizing in their day-to-day roles or to learn new skills. Thus, managers give away some of their employee resources. What do they *get* in return? They are able to leverage talent from elsewhere in the organization to contribute to pressing business challenges they are facing.

This talent could perform roughly the same work employees lent elsewhere would do, or it might be to provide skills the manager needs but doesn't have in the current team. So talent from elsewhere in the company (supply) is acquired in exchange for employees lent elsewhere to learn and apply all of their skills. An employee might have a critical skill set not available from the current team members, a gap that the company would otherwise hire for. By leveraging talent from elsewhere in the organization, the firm saves money; it doesn't have to bring in a contractor, freelancer or consultant to assist on the project or spend resources onboarding someone new. Managers and team members, when working on a new team, enjoy the benefit of using their skills in a new context, learning from others and gaining new skills and perspectives.

In our work with progressive organizations, we have discovered that managers will share talent whether or not incentives are in place to do so. Creative problem-solving results from sharing talent, and lessons learned will continue to have long-term benefit. One company in particular reported significant savings and more customer goodwill, in addition to a marked increase in employee engagement.

THE PRINCIPLE IN ACTION

Let's take a peek at how "You get what you give" works in practice. Juan is a manager of a team of five engineers. His boss has asked him to develop a solution to a vexing problem for one of the company's customers. Juan's team already has a heavy workload trying to innovate one of the firm's current products. The timelines are tight for the special project, and Juan isn't sure his team has the capabilities to succeed. And as is typical, Juan has no budget to bring on a new team member or contractor to help on this—or any—project.

During this high-pressure time, one team member, Kris, asks for permission to participate in a project with another team in a different department where she can learn a new skill related to technology the company is implementing. Juan understands that this initiative is important to her and to the company, so they discuss how work can be shifted to allow Kris one day per week, or a few hours per day, to contribute to the other project. In effect, Juan is "giving his talent away." He does this despite his team's ongoing work assignments and the special project they are in the midst of.

In order to solve the problem his boss has assigned him, Juan realizes he needs to get someone with marketing expertise to help his team better understand the problem that the customer has articulated. He approaches Delana, the marketing manager, to explain the problem, and he asks to borrow talent to work on a solution. Delana says she understands the importance of the project and can see how her team member will gain important insights by working with an engineering team for a brief period. So while Juan has given talent away to another team, he gets talent in return. Thus, he has the right set of skills to solve the problem at hand and provides Kris with an opportunity to learn and grow in an area of rising importance to the company. Furthermore, one of the marketing team members gains perspective from the engineering team that will help her become more successful in the future—a win for everyone.

THE TALENT SCARCITY MINDSET

While "You get what you give" is nice in principle, it is the most challenging shift in prevalent attitudes to overcome when implementing the Inside Gig. This is because most managers operate from a mindset of talent scarcity, a mental model that suggests "These are *my* employees." In other words, "Hands off. Don't touch!"

This may not be a fair portrait of your management style, but companies do ask a great deal of managers. They're given ambitious goals, tight time frames and even tighter budgets. No wonder they aren't willing to part with "their" talent. In fact, they would often be happy to have the talent of other managers as well. The pressure that managers face to achieve their goals despite limited resources creates a mindset of talent scarcity. Budget cuts only exacerbate this tendency. Managers have an ongoing fear that if an employee is lost to a resignation, internal transfer or promotion, there is a significant likelihood the lost position will go unfilled or be eliminated permanently, leaving them to accomplish the same objectives with even fewer people.

The scarcity mindset induces managers to hoard talent. Once they find good employees, they don't want to let them go. Sometimes managers make great hires with particularly valuable skills and don't want to lose them because they have a disproportionate impact on the ability of their teams to meet their goals. In other cases, managers have invested in mentoring, coaching or training employees until their performance is key to team success. Either way, managers value those employees and don't want to see them go elsewhere. While managers may rarely admit to hoarding talent, their actions often speak louder than their words.

Talent hoarders take various actions. They might hold employees down by giving them lower performance ratings than they deserve so that other managers aren't tempted to poach them. More commonly, when employees ask about promotional opportunities, some managers are quick to say, "I think you're doing a great job in your current role, but you aren't quite ready yet for a promotion." Or if the company has a talent review process in which it discusses potential candidates for special developmental opportunities or promotion, talent hoarders become very quiet about their hidden gems. If managers from other departments inquire about having certain employees transferred, talent hoarders often trash-talk those employees to discourage other managers from taking interest in their stars. Over time, managers who hoard talent gain a reputation as people to stay away from because they'll hold employees back in their careers. They are toxic to the organization.

Leaders who are rewarded for producing results but not for promoting people internally have no reason to welcome the prospect of losing high-performing team members to other parts of their companies.

The *2019 Deloitte Human Capital Trends* report indicates that 46 percent of survey respondents say that managers *actively resist* internal mobility.[1] The Institute for Corporate Productivity's (i4cp) talent mobility study of more than 650 global companies found that half of the survey participants (and 74 percent of companies identified as low performers) report that the biggest obstacle to talent mobility rests with managers who refuse to encourage movement.[2]

The talent model that underpins the Inside Gig is antithetical to outdated, bewildering management styles that suppress talent. Even though the talent scarcity mindset is understandable, the business climate has radically changed. This attitude must evolve, too. As organizations compete for scarce talent resources that can make or break their ability to achieve growth plans, holding on to talent within companies is far more important than a manager's desire to keep their team intact.

The innovation that's needed is a shift to a mindset of *abundance* rather than *scarcity* of resources in an organization. When managers and team leaders let go of ownership of their talent, it is liberating for everyone. This more inclusive attitude helps managers look beyond their own employee groups to solve problems, and allows their employees to explore passions and interests across other groups, teams or departments. This sense of being "boundaryless" as an organization enhances a firm's ability to innovate.

Different disciplines have their own methods of approaching and solving problems. What possibilities could arise when a customer-facing rep is asked about her thoughts on a supply-chain issue, or a marketing employee is seconded by an engineering department? You'll never know until you try. But it is a truism that when you examine challenges from different perspectives or with another set of tools, you shine a light on answers that might not previously have been considered. New skill sets can also be brought to issues, adding value and enhancing work products to make them more valuable to consumers. A culture that considers all talent as a company asset and allows and expects people to move seamlessly across the organization will build employees who are well rounded, understand the firm as a whole and have perspectives broader than those focused on a single function.

TALENT MOBILITY

Talent mobility has traditionally been defined as shifting talent around to promote further employee development. For large global companies, this usually meant assigning employees projects to build global competence. Given the complexities of today's business world, organizations frequently try to move people laterally to boost their breadth of perspective. Talent mobility both increases the visibility of employees within the company and exposes such employees to new experiences (new managers, countries, markets, functions or sub-functions), greatly improving overall competence. In today's networked and knowledge-based business environment, establishing relationships across an organization and enhancing employees' wider understanding of the inner workings of either a function or the company as a whole delivers considerable value to the firm as well as to the employees themselves. This is particularly true when cultivating versatile leaders to handle diverse functions. Furthermore, the need to retain and develop top talent grows especially important to organizations as it becomes more difficult to hire the right employees to achieve business priorities.

Talent mobility improves levels of employee engagement by allowing people the opportunity to move around within an organization to foster new skills, be exposed to stimulating experiences and prove themselves. To fuel a company's growth, talent mobility is needed to keep employees learning and engaged in order to retain them, as well as to build a broader understanding of the business, enhance overall organization performance and achieve competitive advantage. Given rising talent shortages, the approach of simply hiring new talent when demand increases or a different skill set is needed doesn't work as well as it once did.

Deloitte's 2019 Global Human Capital Trends report shows that 20 percent of C-suite leaders (executive-level managers who often have "chief" in their title) rate talent mobility as one of the top three most urgent issues for their companies, while 76 percent of survey respondents rated it as important for their organizations.[3] This is largely because many companies are experiencing historically low unemployment rates and a growing skills shortage. To make matters worse, only 15 percent of global employees are engaged at work, an amazing level of wasted potential.[4] Interestingly enough, while only 10 percent of the workforce in Western Europe is engaged, 33 percent of the U.S. workforce is engaged. This suggests that management practices are providing a competitive advantage to U.S. employers, although they, too, are leaving a great deal of worker productivity on the table.

CASE STUDY: THE GAP INC.

Let's look at how one company Edie Goldberg consulted with cultivated an appreciation for the importance of internal talent mobility to develop the general management or strategic leaders needed to run it. In 2003, the chief financial officer (CFO) of Gap Inc. realized that most of the professionals in his organization were developing themselves as specialists. For instance, when employees joined the tax sub-function of finance, the next career moves they considered were the subsequent steps up the tax corporate ladder. Such an employee went from being a tax analyst, to a manager of tax, to a senior manager, then director, and finally a vice president of tax. Employees didn't naturally think about rotating through the various sub-functions within finance (e.g., financial planning and analysis, tax, treasury, investor relations). Most of Gap Inc.'s finance employees were becoming deep specialists within their own sub-functions. As a result, when one of the Gap Inc. brands (Gap, Old Navy, Banana Republic, etc.) needed a CFO, it had to hire talent externally; none of its employees had the broad expertise required to fill the position. This caused a significant morale and retention issue, since employees felt they would never be considered for such important leadership positions.

Edie was asked to help Gap Inc. find a solution, which led to the creation of Shaping Your Future Gap Inc., a career management program that defined the lateral career moves necessary to become a finance generalist and indicated a career web (rather than ladder or path) that showed the various routes one could take to achieve individual career goals—such as CFO (generalist) rather than head of tax (specialist). Managers were trained to have career conversations using the new tools, and corporate leadership set the expectation that talent mobility was essential to build the broad leaders the company needed to fill senior leadership positions.

After an employee has been in their role for two years (the first for learning, the second for mastery), their manager has a career conversation that strongly encourages changes in internal assignments based on the employee's career goals. If employees would like to become a CFO one day, they're moved to different sub-functions within finance or outside the finance function to gain broader business experience. If they're interested in becoming a deep specialist, then a rotation to another role that builds deeper expertise within the sub-function is recommended. As a consequence, Gap Inc. has been able to build the leadership bench strength needed to promote from within, which has helped to engage and retain finance talent.[5]

THE BENEFITS OF THE BOUNDARYLESS ORGANIZATION

In chapter 2 on the Fourth Industrial Revolution, we touched on continuous learning as an aspect of the new employment contract. If there is one thing that is well understood about millennials, it is that this generation, more than any before it, thrives on change and on learning on demand. Maybe that's because they were born during a time when everything changes quickly and the half-life of skills is plunging. For business success, you must create a continuous learning culture. In fact, on most employee opinion surveys, the lowest-scoring item is satisfaction with career development. This is most likely the result of people working so hard that they can't "take the time" for learning. The Inside Gig can be a vehicle for on-the-job learning in small bites. Whether employees apply their skills with a new group of people (where they're learning from others and broadening their perspectives), use their skills in a new context (deepening their understanding of their skill sets), or work on a project slightly larger than they've experienced before and take on new responsibilities, the Inside Gig gives employees opportunities for continuous learning. Both "giving" talent and "getting" talent in return deliver learning and growth for all employees involved.

In today's hyper-competitive talent market, it's essential to give employees opportunities to spread their wings and try something new or employ underutilized skills so that they feel more purpose and meaning at work. Competition for talent is one of the top challenges facing companies today, ahead of compensation.[6] So a crucial element of any talent strategy is to find ways to offer employees the experiences they value; otherwise, they are liable to leave to find them elsewhere.

When people use the term *internal talent mobility*, they're generally referring to moving talent to different jobs within an organization for the purpose of supplying specific learning opportunities. However, as we saw in this chapter, managers resist moving talent internally because often the people who are identified for these rotational assignments are the organization's best and brightest—exactly the talent managers want to hold on to in order to meet their own goals. By applying the Inside Gig's principles, there is an opportunity to consider talent mobility in a wider, more flexible manner. Rather than completely moving from a *job* to take on a new challenge or apply skills in a different context, what if you think about work as a series of projects and make room for one *project* that's outside an employee's day-to-day job responsibilities? Might those learning experiences be more palatable to managers who don't want to lose their best talent?

We're not suggesting that the Inside Gig will completely replace traditional internal talent mobility. There is a great deal of value to be gained from taking an international assignment or moving to a new role in a different function. But when employees can continuously learn and grow through smaller micro-learning experiences while doing real work, perhaps it will change the mindset of managers to see the abundance of talent available to them to solve problems for specific projects.

Is a talent marketplace based on projects more acceptable than having employees completely leave their jobs to gain experiences elsewhere in the company, or worse, in another company? Clearly, we think the answer is yes!

PERSPECTIVES FROM THE INSIDE GIG

The Employee

The "You get what you give" practice speaks to the employee experience. It is all about managers giving employees opportunities to explore projects outside their teams. Releasing employees from some responsibilities by rethinking how work gets done or by reallocating part of their responsibilities to others allows those employees to learn something new or use currently underutilized expertise elsewhere in the company. Employees can bring their holistic selves to work and experience the value of *all* of the expertise and experience they can offer their company.

Plus, employees are given a safe place to stretch and learn, to work on projects in which they lend their expertise while learning new skills from others. Employees may also get opportunities to pursue work they find meaningful or are passionate about because of its application in the world. When employees work on projects they are passionate about, they work harder and are more focused, which helps to create meaning at work. All of these factors are likely to result in employees wanting to stay with their company, because they value the experiences they get there.

Employees are also provided with choice in the projects they wish to pursue based on personal needs and not just the needs of their managers. By working on projects outside the realm of their day-to-day job responsibilities, employees are given more diversity in their work, which is a key factor for employee engagement. No one enjoys being stuck doing the same type of work over and over again.

The Manager

Managers have a lot on their plates and are held accountable for the total performance of their teams. However, managers often don't have the skills or capabilities, or even capacity, on their teams to accomplish important goals. While the "You get what you give" principle does require managers to give employees opportunities to spread their wings and try something new, managers get a lot in return. For example, they may get an employee from elsewhere in the organization who can provide needed skills or experiences. This might increase the capacity of the team or facilitate the speed with which it can get a project done because it has the right expertise to do the work.

Further, by providing employees with opportunities to try new and different things, to learn new skills that are important to their careers, managers are able to retain those employees longer. Unlike in traditional talent mobility, we aren't suggesting that managers completely give up an employee for the greater good of the company and that employee's career growth. Instead, we are proposing that managers give employees some space, maybe as little as 10 percent to 20 percent of their time, to explore other areas of the business, build new relationships, learn new skills or use skills they have but that aren't required for their day-to-day jobs. We know from experience that when employees get stuck in jobs doing the same things over and over again, they may get bored and quit to take on new challenges elsewhere. Rather than lose employees completely, by giving them space, managers have at least a chance of holding on to them longer. The worst thing that might happen is that the employee finds another part of the organization where they fit better. But that is far better than having them jump to another company that better meets their needs.

The Company

When an organization leverages the talent it has within the company, rather than hiring freelancers, contractors or consultants to do that work, there are significant cost savings. Today, organizations don't have a way to optimize existing talent and leverage all the collective capabilities of their talent supply. Employees bring with them a rich set of experiences and skills from prior employment settings. However, organizational structures aren't designed to utilize these full ranges of skills. They are designed to merely utilize the skills for which employees were hired. New technological advancements make it possible to match the right talent to the right opportunities within companies, which allows the full capacity of talent to be unleashed to work on the business problems at hand. It enables organizations to shift resources to higher-priority projects and staff those projects in a matter of hours or days rather than weeks or months. Such an ability has an impact on the bottom line: it will increase productivity and lower overall costs for the organization.

Additional benefits accrue to the organization. Prior research has shown that innovative, employee-focused HR practices, such as the Inside Gig, lead to more engaged employees. Engaged employees lead to increased customer satisfaction, which leads to market growth and higher revenues. Retention becomes less of an issue.[7]

KEY TAKEAWAYS

- Principle no. 1, "You get what you give," addresses how talent sharing across departments or functions is a better way to optimize resources. Managers commit to giving their people time to participate in projects outside their teams. Sure, they are giving away some of their employee resources, but in return, they get valuable talent from elsewhere in the organization to contribute to pressing business challenges on their plate. This talent could entail performing roughly the same work employees lent elsewhere would do (providing a learning experience for someone else), or it might be to provide skills managers need but don't have in their current teams.

- Implementing this innovative practice requires managers to shift from a mindset of talent scarcity ("my employees") to a mindset of abundance ("all of the employees in the company").

- An organization that considers all talent a company asset and facilitates employees moving seamlessly across the organization from project to project will have employees who are well rounded and have broader perspectives than just their single functions.

- The term *internal talent mobility* generally refers to moving talent to different jobs within the organization in order to supply specific learning opportunities. The Inside Gig approach to talent management presents a new way to consider talent mobility in a more flexible manner. Rather than completely moving from a *job* to take on a new challenge or to apply skills in a different context, perhaps employees can simply make room for one *project* that's outside their day-to-day job responsibilities.

- In this era of historic low unemployment and low employee engagement, the growing skills shortage poses a vexing challenge for organizations. By building talent mobility practices that foster skill development and increase employee engagement, companies can build the talent they can't buy in the marketplace.

REFLECTION POINTS

Do you think employees should be able to contribute the skills they have elsewhere in the organization on a part-time or temporary basis?

Do you think your team could benefit from other perspectives?

When it comes to talent, do you think your company's culture has a scarcity mindset or an abundance mindset? Or is it somewhere along the spectrum?

Would you agree or disagree that innovating talent mobility could have an impact on attracting new hires and retaining your people?

CHAPTER 4
Principle No. 2: Know What You Have

Who looks outside dreams, who looks inside awakes.
—Carl Jung

IMAGINE SOME OF THE CONSEQUENCES if the chief operating officer (COO) of a company were unable to provide an accurate inventory of its capital assets. Operations would suffer, decision-making would be constrained, and the development and execution of strategic plans would be fraught with risk. Now consider this: How many HR executives can provide an accurate inventory of their organizations' talent assets? Furthermore, what consequences does this lack of information create for companies? Here are some possibilities:

- increased hiring costs to fill skill gaps
- inability to accurately match people's skills with project assignments
- lengthy cycle times for product development and release
- a widespread belief that badly needed skill sets are nowhere to be found in the company
- inadequate career development because internal opportunities and inventories of employees' skills are not known

Conversely, imagine what might be possible if an accurate, real-time inventory of skill assets was available to your company. What would the benefits be to hiring managers? to project leaders? to workforce planning professionals? The potential impact could be enormous, and operational executives are paying attention. As Randall Stephenson, CEO of AT&T, recently asked his leadership team, "Do we have the skills we need to win in our business?"[1]

In *The Future-Proof Workplace*, Linda Sharkey and Morag Barrett state: "Companies need to invest in every person to ensure that everyone can deliver on innovation. Which skills are required to achieve our strategy? Who has them now, and who needs to develop expertise?"[2] Clearly, the role of talent in the success equation for sustainable companies has finally reached center stage.

THINK OF SKILL ASSETS AS CAPITAL ASSETS

By now it should be abundantly clear that the world has changed. Today, everyone is talking about competitive advantage.[3] We argue that the new competitive advantage is rooted in knowing the skills you have now, intelligently deploying them, and hiring for the skill gaps you have identified. To intelligently deploy available skills against business requirements, you need to develop an accurate inventory of the talent supply that comprises a workforce. In the book *Victory through Organization*, the authors write: "Labor economists have known for years that over time, major competitors will have roughly the same raw, specialized talent; therefore, the competitive advantage is what you do with the talent you have."[4] This raises the crucial question for every organization today: *Do we currently have an accurate and comprehensive skills inventory of our workforce?* Recall what Albert Einstein taught us when he said we can't use the same type of thinking to solve problems as the thinking that was used to create them. When you start to consider skill assets in the same way as you do capital assets, you create the conditions for a different way to think about why it's important to develop skills inventories.

ENTER THE TALENT SUPPLY CHAIN

The supply chain is often referred to when the topic is the manufacturing of a product, but the term is rarely used when referring to talent inside organizations. The term *supply chain* was defined as a network between a company and its suppliers to produce and distribute a specific product to the final buyer. This network includes different activities, people, entities, information and resources. Throughout the last three industrial revolutions, the term has been used to describe the supply and demand of goods and services; however, you can also think of the inventory of talent in much the same way.

In this book, we use the term *talent supply chain* as the inventory of available talent resources in an organization (or talent supply) against the demand for work. As more and more businesses rely on knowledge workers, the correlations between supply chains for products or goods will be similar to the supply chain for talent. As the Fourth Industrial Revolution continues, skilled workers will continue to be a scarce resource that is in demand. The law of economics suggests that scarcity of supply drives more demand. If skilled and specialized talent will continue to be in high demand, companies will need to have a strategy to ensure (much like in product supply chains) that their inventory of skilled talent is never depleted to such an extent that the company cannot achieve its goals. The innovative practices that inform the Inside Gig are designed to mitigate such a risk.

Maintaining a Skills Inventory

As we saw in chapter 3, Principle No. 1: You Get What You Give, so much of the strategic value for a company's talent operating model is related to managing its "core capabilities," since without them the execution of the strategy is at risk. Many companies today realize that having an accurate inventory of skills is a source of competitive advantage. By knowing what they have and what they don't have, they can manage their supply, set strategies to reskill, and close gaps. What CHROs are now tasked with is becoming the COO of the talent supply chain—it's their job to know what's in the inventory and to effectively manage the ebb and flow of critical skills *before* those skill sets are irrelevant or urgent. More than ever, CEOs rely on their CHROs to manage one of the most valuable resources—the talent to win.

With skills having a shelf life of three to five years and the rise of machine automation, many of these skill sets will need to evolve. So how can CHROs become better at knowing what they have, predicting what talent needs are coming, and preparing those who manage the work for which skills can be cultivated on the inside? Without a crystal ball, there will need to be ways to get the insights early enough to ensure that talent strategies are in line with the business. And although CEOs have long been saying that human resources are the greatest asset, it's now more of a reality than ever before.

In a 2017 article titled "Harnessing Revolution: Creating the Future Workforce," published by Accenture's strategy team, the authors describe the top three actions all companies need to take now in terms of their talent supply chains to remain competitive and prepare for the future workforce:

1. **Accelerate reskilling:** Ensure that your workers recognize the skills required for the future and begin planning transitions that will inevitably come with the digital age.

2. **Redesign work to unlock human potential:** Prepare for more flexible work models, including project-based assignments and gig workers.

3. **Strengthen the talent pipeline from its source:** Prepare for multiple generations at once and collaborate across academia, industries and government to reformulate the curricula and create a future-ready talent pipeline.

Further, the article states, "The Fourth Industrial Revolution con-tributed to an imbalance in the global economy. New jobs are being created that require skills that don't yet exist at scale. Companies need to increase the speed of reskilling. Positioning their organization, and their people, to win in this newest revolution. Or risk leaving entire generations of workers without work or the skills to acquire it, destabilizing the lives of individuals and society at large."[5] So, clearly, the issue of managing a supply chain of existing skills, while focusing on the needs of the future, will become increasingly more important.

CASE STUDY: SEAGATE TECHNOLOGY

Managing existing skills with an eye on the future is exactly the challenge John Cleveland, former CHRO of Seagate Technology, was solving. The company is reshaping its footprint in response to dynamic changes in its industry. As the industry, company and road map change, Seagate is preparing its 42,000-strong workforce to meet the future need. By identifying latent knowledge and creating experiences for employees that encourage them to follow their passions for personal and professional growth, Seagate is demonstrating the innovative growth mindset this book encourages. Seagate has developed a talent marketplace that is a strategic differentiator for the company, enabling it to build an agile and engaged workforce from the inside out.

Seagate found it had programs that were developed in response to business needs (e.g., internal development programs, talent reviews, skill-based pay, online access to courses and tuition reimbursement), but not an overall strategy to create an environment of learning where employees own their development and become more valuable to Seagate in response to the changing markets. Organizationally, Seagate combined the internal mobility team with the learning/development team and creating a new leadership role to "own" the creation of a talent marketplace.

To support employees' growth and the positive impact on the company, the leadership mindset is shifting from the perspective of "these are my employees" to "all employees are Seagate employees." The role of leaders is to manage talent and facilitate the opportunities that employees are given to grow personally and professionally, wherever that may be at Seagate. Other basic headwinds, such as the budgeting process and job requisitions, are being addressed as roadblocks to the flow of talent.

Seagate's talent marketplace crosses over many of the traditional HR centers of excellence and silos, and it requires a different way to look at employee development. It is a culture shift to an environment where leaders make it possible for employees to own their careers. Creating a talent marketplace could be a once-in-a-career opportunity for HR to support an agile workforce.

Today, there are relatively few options to inventory the skills in your organization and keep the inventory current. Until recently, the only way to inventory skills was to run assessments of your talent through management calibration sessions against competencies by each role. Not only was this inefficient, but the competencies often became irrelevant quickly or were too generic to zero in on the potential relevance of specific skills to other roles that an individual could seek out within the organization. SAP, WorkDay and Oracle—the three biggest HCM vendors—just began to pivot in this direction after realizing that skills were the future and had more levels of specificity than competencies.

Making Skills Visible

In a 2017 article "Why Companies Need to Build a Skills Inventory," Jeff Hesse notes: "CEOs told us that finding the skills they need has become the biggest challenge to their business."[6] As companies are pressed to manage growing demand for a flexible workforce—both on-demand workers or "gig work" on the outside and project-based work on the inside—their ability to visualize an inventory of skills will be important for those who manage and assign the work. The traditional leadership model, where work was centralized to one manager or leader who had to acquire those skills for a job, no longer suits the new workplace. People must acquire skills for projects of short duration, so they must acquire those skills quickly. If a manager or project leader has a way to visualize a future demand on their skills inventory, ramp-up time is lessened.

CASE STUDY: THE RISE OF DATA SCIENCE AND SKILLS VISUALIZATION

With the rise of data science has come the ability to visualize and analyze data in new ways. This includes skills across both industries and talent pools. Some of the companies we spoke with during our research have started to find new ways to gain insights from skills visualization data. At HERE Technologies, for example, the Talent Platform team and HR partnered with data scientists and data visualization specialists to find out if they could visualize what skill sets might be emerging within the company, specifically among the software engineering pool globally. HR wanted to know how many of their engineers had like or different skill sets. Additionally, they wanted to find out if visualizing those skills could tell help them understand, among their engineers with machine learning capability, what skills were most correlated and what new skills, if any, might be emerging.

The exercise indicated that among those engineers with machine learning skills, there was also a skill set showing up around Python. The HR team started to review the profiles of engineers with like skills and correlated those profiles to the demand for that skill set that was showing up in their internal talent marketplace for projects and in current full-time roles. HR discovered that there were approximately 35 engineers who had similar skills or a profile of similar skills. Given the demand for more of this skill in the company, the HR team created a plan to proactively reach out to those engineers and ask if they might be interested in computer visualization. Out of the 35 engineers, almost half were interested to do some upskilling in computer visualization / data visualization. Thus, the company had a strategy to create more supply of this critical skill set simply by being able to leverage skill visibility to inform their talent strategy.

This concept of using data science and skills visualization to determine a talent supply chain is based on two assumptions. The first is that many of the individual and team capabilities required to support critical business goals and objectives are already present in the current workforce of most organizations. Indeed, while a larger inventory of skills than is being utilized is present in these companies, an accurate accounting of those skill sets is at best unclear.

The second assumption is that future business requirements may or may not be clearly understood. There are many reasons for this. What is clear, however, is that this lack of clarity, coupled with the challenges of skill identification, inventory building and intelligent deployment of talent assets creates a serious issue for companies. They will be ill-prepared for future challenges that are sure to require some new mix of skill sets. Furthermore, the absence of an accurate inventory of talent in any company greatly reduces its ability to provide employees with targeted and meaningful development opportunities. The consequence is that employees leave their jobs, as we explore below.

In their 2018 McKinsey article "Right-Skilling for Your Future Workforce," Emily Ross, Bill Schaninger and Emily Seng Yue note that by 2030 as many as 375 million workers globally will have to master fresh skills as their current jobs evolve alongside the rise of automation and machine capabilities. The study goes on to state that to build a competitive workforce of the future proactively, you must gain clarity on today's workforce gaps and the future skills needed.[7]

THE RISE OF INTELLIGENT ASSET MANAGEMENT

The Power of Matching the Job/Task to the Right Person/Skills

Recent survey data suggest that only 33 percent of U.S. employees are engaged with their jobs, and that a high percentage of employees would leave their jobs for what they perceive are better ones.[8] There's widespread agreement that employees who are more engaged are more deeply invested in the work they're doing. They demonstrate higher levels of performance and satisfaction, and that is a direct result of effectively matching their skills with job or project requirements.[9] Said another way, when people's skills are more accurately matched to work/project requirements, performance and job satisfaction improve.

When employees state that they would leave their current jobs for "better ones," compensation is generally one of the motivators. However, survey data repeatedly show that there are other factors associated with the willingness to leave.[10] One of those factors is professional development. Employees want more opportunities to utilize and strengthen the skills they already possess, as well as on-the-job experiences to learn new ones.

These facts present not only a challenge for companies, but also a strategic opportunity. The opportunity is that if organizations adopt data science and visualization methods that more accurately match employee skill sets to business requirements, they should expect to see improvements in productivity and engagement levels. For employees, the opportunity is that it enables them to tap into their greatest talent passions and capabilities, to further their professional development, and to increase the value their work brings to their companies. The obvious next questions should be: How do organizations accomplish this? And what information is necessary to achieve the desired outcomes?

The simplest answer is to use intelligent methods of collecting relevant skill and experience information, then match and deploy available talent to business requirements. On one level, this is literally a case of supply and demand, which requires an ability to accurately determine both parts of that equation. On a deeper level, however, the question is: How does my company tap into the vast untapped potential inherent in our workforce? And perhaps more importantly: What are the business consequences of "untapped" workforce potential?

To provide some perspective, this is what untapped workforce potential might look like:

• Individuals and teams function at only acceptable or marginal levels of performance, but are unable to reach true high-performance levels.

• Companies are unable to provide work experiences that truly motivate people and surface their deepest levels of passion and commitment.

• The number of urgent actions is continuously increased, without a process that matches performance and motivation potential with the activities that result in the highest return on investment (ROI).

67

• Employees utilize only a portion of their total skill assets while companies are unable to fill skill gaps for projects and other assignments.

Many senior executives, scholars and authors are expressing their view that in today's business environment, the differentiating factor between successful companies and those that fail is less and less contingent on the product or services they provide and more contingent on how they manage their talent assets. Indeed, in the article "Technology and Intellectual Capital: The New Revolution," Richard Mirabile states that "the distinctive competitive advantage of world class organizations in the future will ultimately reside with the collection, management, and distribution of talent."[11]

Technology today offers a possibility that was not available just a few years ago: the capability to quickly create and provide access to comprehensive, accurate descriptions of workforce talent. With immediate access to information of this type, decisions can be made faster—and today, speed matters. Decision makers can now leverage skills inventory information as a form of operational excellence. Faster access to more complete and accurate information can lead to such outcomes as these:

• reduced cycle time to staff projects
• reduced cycle time to complete projects
• reduced cycle time to develop products and services and bring them to market
• reduced cycle time to revenue generation via new product or service deployment
• higher levels of employee engagement
• higher levels of job or career satisfaction
• reduced turnover rates, resulting in fewer hiring replacements

These kinds of benefits, in turn, translate into lower operating costs, faster time to revenue production, higher employee retention and the foundation for a healthy corporate culture.

The power of a readily deployable technology lies in its ability to compress the time frames required to collect and distribute relevant information, then to rapidly deploy the right talent to the right situation. In this case, that information is both opportunity-based—*What is the work that needs to be done?*—and talent-based—*What is the total inventory of skills that exist in the company that is available to perform the work?*

Davis Carlin and Bill Schaninger sum it up in another McKinsey report, "Matching the Right Talent to the Right Roles," as follows: "While talent matching is challenging, when it's done right, rapidly and at scale by a large organization, the outcome can prove to be a significant performance differentiator. Based on our research, these organizations outperform competitors 2-to-1."[12]

The Balance Sheet of Talent Assets

In the near future, there will be balance sheets for the talent assets of a company and new calculations will be created to identify their real valuations for investors, shareholders and employees. These collective capabilities—the knowledge, skills and experiences of a workforce—when managed effectively, can result in higher levels of productivity and performance output.

We recommend that intelligent talent asset management should become a core competency of every organization. Once that becomes standard operating procedure—that is, a fundamental way of doing business—it can be leveraged into a competitive advantage by identifying and strategically deploying the collective expertise of the existing workforce. Greg Case, CEO of AON, has stated, "Pure capital allocation is essential, but that's not enough. People allocation is as powerful as financial allocation. Do we have the right talent in place and how should we think about talent development?"[13]

In the McKinsey report "Right-Skilling for Your Future Workforce," the authors discuss what's needed to build a competitive workforce of the future. They state that right-skilling requires: 1) gaining clarity on today's workforce gaps and the future skills needed; 2) a robust plan to supply the future demand; and 3) rapid, disciplined execution.[14]

Asking the Right Questions

Asking the right questions will almost always lead to more innovative solutions, to new ways of thinking and problem solving. In the case of talent strategies, asking the right questions opens the door to exploring the strategic impact of workforce talent. How can you tap into the enormous performance and motivation potential that lies untapped in your workforce? This is the "secret" part of the sauce that is yet to be discovered. This is the next big thing.

To emphasize the point, ask yourself how you and your company would answer these two questions: What would it take to unlock even a small amount of the untapped performance and motivation potential of your workforce? And, if the contributions of your workforce could be increased by only 10 percent, what would the impact be to the business?

Make no mistake, this is not to suggest that increasing employee workloads is the formula for higher productivity levels. Being busy doesn't necessarily provide increases in performance. Research out of Stanford University and other institutions supports the conclusion that working long hours does not translate to higher productivity levels.[15] The challenge today is to use intelligent methods to identify, match and deploy available talent to business requirements that best connect to employees' motivators. As we've discussed above, it is literally a case of supply and demand.

Imagine the possibilities of combining a truly intelligent talent strategy with a well-planned business strategy. As measured by productivity improvements, reductions in employee turnover, cost savings from not needing to hire and onboard new employees, product and service cycle time reductions, increases in innovation, and higher levels of team performance, the ROI could be significant. These are only the most obvious indicators of the potential impact; there are likely others.

The most innovative and progressive companies are those that explore new ways of working and new business models. By operationalizing the parts that work best for their particular set of circumstances and then evolving them into core business processes, they create the conditions for a competitive advantage. The cost of not innovating in today's economy is likely to be stagnation, or worse, missed opportunities for expansion and growth. As the old saying goes, if you keep doing the same things, expect to get the same results.

PERSPECTIVES FROM THE INSIDE GIG

The Employee

Employees rarely have opportunities to demonstrate their complete range and depth of skills. Because jobs have been created with specific descriptions and accountabilities, workers have generally been expected to perform against those guidelines, but not much more. The methods that have been developed to match people to jobs have resulted in many benefits, but they come at a cost—the lack of visibility into a broader, potentially more valuable set of capabilities that remain untapped or underutilized. New ideas on the future of work combined with growing pressures for companies to remain competitive are changing the way talent is integrated into business operations and strategies. The emergence of data science and skills visibility is opening up new opportunities for all employees.

The Manager

It's essential that managers have a complete and accurate inventory of their company's talent supply chain. Without it, they are forced to manage projects with unnecessary restrictions and incomplete information. Knowing the skill sets required to perform work and knowing what talent capabilities exist in the company are competitive advantages when it comes to project completion and product development. Indeed, business goals can only be achieved by knowing what talent is required to accomplish the desired results. Managers must have this information readily accessible if they are to deliver on their goals and objectives. "Know what you have" is the key ingredient for deploying the right person with the right skills at the right time.

The Company

It's time for companies to consider talent assets in the same way that they consider financial and capital assets. Not having robust talent inventories can lead to constrained decision-making, project and product release delays, unnecessary hiring costs and roadblocks in executing strategic plans. Conversely, developing and maintaining an accurate talent inventory can accelerate innovation efforts, shorten project and product development cycles, and improve engagement levels and retention of key employees. Companies are being forced to rethink how work is structured, and consequently, they must also take a fresh look at the total availability of talent they have on their balance sheets. The ability to fully understand the breadth of the talent supply chain feeds the pipeline of accurately and rapidly matching people and work, surely a formula for success.

KEY TAKEAWAYS

- The gig economy will require a mindset shift in how organizations think about talent mobility and deployment. The concept of a talent supply chain enables operational leaders to use the kind of thinking that they use for capital goods and supply chains that are embedded in their ways of doing business.

- Successful talent strategies must include the ability to build accurate and comprehensive inventories of the knowledge, skills and experiences of the workforce. New technologies simplify the complexities of this task and provide real-time snapshots of talent availability matched against business requirements.

- The recent emergence of data science and skills visualization provide the kind of rigor needed to adapt to the gig economy and to the new ways of working that are becoming necessary for companies to maintain competitive advantages in their markets.

• The "secret sauce" of sustainable companies lies in their willingness and ability to access the untapped hidden potential inherent in their workforces. Most companies are sitting on a deep repository of hidden talent and unfulfilled motivations, and the possibilities resulting from unleashing this resource are yet to be realized.

REFLECTION POINTS

Have you or your company thought in terms of a talent supply chain as a way to solve skill gaps?

Do you think your company does a good, fair or poor job of managing talent assets and matching the job or task at hand to the right person with the right skill set?

Are you of a view that talent in your organization should be mobile?

Do you have data to suggest that underutilizing employees is causing a retention problem?

Do you think science and data can help predict future roles and strengthen your company's talent pool?

CHAPTER 5
Principle No. 3: Create a Learning Organization

We now accept the fact that learning is a lifelong process of keeping abreast
of change. And the most pressing task is to teach people how to learn.
—Peter Drucker

IMAGINE THAT YOUR COMPANY IS INVESTING in a new manufacturing
technology that will further its growth and make it more competitive.
The challenge is to reskill workers and bring the new technology on-
stream as quickly as possible. Leadership had prepared for such an
eventuality and ensured that employees were given opportunities to
learn and develop. Employees are allowed to explore new career possibilities within the company, while still benefiting from the security of
their current job. Managers have created high-performing teams that
are able to adapt as technologies change the work they need to perform. The company sees change as opportunity. This is a learning
culture at its finest.

What you do not need to imagine is the reality of the workplace
today. With the demand for new skills combined with a tight talent
marketplace, jobs are left unfilled for long periods. The only way for
companies to overcome this challenge is to build the skills themselves,
rather than waiting to find this precious talent in the open talent
marketplace. According to a Deloitte study of almost 10,000 respondents across the globe, the top issue of focus for most organizations
is the need to change the way people learn.[1] Past ways of learning are

not practical for today's globally distributed organizations. And traditional approaches to learning have rarely led to significant changes in behavior.

Sadly, despite what researchers have known about training for decades, most organizations do not benefit by teaching employees new skills or information, either because these skills lack application in the workplace or because the organization does not have the infrastructure to support the application of new skills. Typically, training programs are assessed in terms of how people feel after the training (Reaction), or sometimes at the end of training by a knowledge-acquisition test (Learning). But rarely is the effectiveness of training measured in terms of behavioral change back in the workplace (Behavior), or better yet, the achievement of improved results because of training (Results or Return on Investment).[2] Despite the evidence that we need to change *how* we learn in organizations, the race to acquire new skills is compounding our methodological deficiencies.

At the same time, a significant shift is underway regarding how individuals provide proof of their expertise. In the past, an employee could rely on a college degree or diploma as evidence of a certain level of knowledge or capability. Over time, years of work experience also served as a measure of an individual's level of expertise in a given field. But today, the skill sets are shifting so quickly that what was learned in school or on the job no longer implies expertise in new and emerging skill sets. Certifications and credentialing of skill domains are emerging as proof of expertise. So, as we move from the jobs economy to the skills economy, having an outside source certify that a specific level of expertise has been obtained is becoming the way future employees will market themselves to potential new employers. Certifications can be industry-specific (e.g., human resources, project management), software-specific (e.g., Salesforce, Google AdWords), or domain-specific (e.g., Python, UX Design).

This chapter explores the future of learning in the gig economy and how your company can create a learning organization.

THE RESKILLING REVOLUTION

Creative destruction is accelerating the pace of change in the corporate landscape. Today, it is estimated that given the current rate of change in the companies in the S&P 500, there will be between a 50 percent and 75 percent change in the companies listed in this index.[3] That is an enormous amount of change! Business model disruption is creating new industries, displacing companies on the S&P 500, and new companies are scaling up quickly based on new and emerging technologies. Think about Uber (and its competitors) disrupting the taxi industry. Or better yet, consider the major pivot Amazon has made from online book seller to seller of anything and everything, disrupting not only the retail markets, but also traditional delivery services such as the U.S. Postal Service and United Parcel Service (UPS). The fast pace of innovation is bringing us new technologies that enable companies to do things they could never do before. Sixty percent of companies are investing in new technologies; however, only 3 percent of those organizations are investing in employee training.[4]

The workforce is not prepared for this change, and companies have not been investing in reskilling their employees to keep pace. Companies are primarily investing in reskilling high-wage earners, but the data tell us that the jobs most likely to be affected through technological disruption are lower skilled. Companies that think they are going to hire their way through this challenge should think again! The talent simply is not available.

CASE STUDY: CISCO SYSTEMS

One company that is investing in reskilling its employees is Cisco Systems. Cisco has transformed its business model, moving away from its core server technologies to a new focus on the Internet of Things. How does a company deal with this significant change in skill sets? Once upon a time, a company making a shift like this would have laid off employees with server skills that are of decreasing importance to the company and then hired new employees with expertise in IoT. But there is a small problem with this strategy: finding sufficient people with the necessary skill set to effect the transformation. Thus, Cisco decided that it needed a way to give its people the opportunity to learn the skills that the company needs, while they continued with their current work. Cisco had to find out exactly what skills its employees had. Up to this point, the company had little more than job titles in a database. This data did not provide the information the company needed to determine who had foundational skills that they could build upon to develop the new capabilities the company needed.

Cisco Systems created an internal opportunity platform, where people could opt in to small project assignments where they would gain more exposure to IoT projects. While employees did have to take these assignments on in addition to their day-to-day jobs, they knew that these projects would help them to be more employable in the future when the company completed its transformation to an IoT company.

It is obvious from the Cisco Systems example that learning agility will become the key skill set for the future. As positions change due to technological advancements, individuals need to be able to learn new skills and change as their roles change.

The perceived importance of learning quickly is demonstrated by the fact that Manpower Group developed a Learnability Quotient[5] to help individuals assess their learning styles. Manpower defines *learnability* as "the desire and ability to quickly grow and adapt to new circumstances and challenges throughout your work life."[6] The idea behind the Learnability Quotient is to help individuals understand their own learning profile. After completing the assessment, a report is generated that provides users with their learning profile and a variety of resources to improve their learnability. Organizations can benefit from understanding their employees' Learnability Quotient because it is an indicator of learning agility and helps gauge if individuals are motivated to learn on their own.

THE 100-YEAR LIFE

The need for people to become agile learners goes beyond the current digital transformation that most organizations are experiencing. It impacts the personal arc of our lives. Many of us still assume that we will spend the first part of our life going to school, then work until we are 65, and then retire. This life model no longer works. Between 1900 and 2000, life expectancy in the U.S. increased by 60 percent for men and by 63 percent for women.[7] Thus, in the not-so-distant future, many people will live to be 100 years old. In their book *The 100-Year Life*, Lynda Gratton and Andrew Scott from the London Business School discuss the breakdown of our traditional life model.[8] It will not be possible to retire at 65, because most of us will not have enough retirement savings to sustain us in old age. Furthermore, today's 65-year-old is like yesterday's 50-year-old—healthier and more vital. The book focuses on quality of life in the "extra years" we have. The authors suggest reframing "What will we do when we are older?" to "How can we be younger for longer?" This requires us to pay attention to fitness, skills and relationships. They also suggest that the education we get when we are younger cannot possibly carry us through our entire lifespan. We will need to retool over time. While they did not write this book especially about this digital age, the idea of needing to retool throughout one's life is even truer today.

 Learning agility *is the ability to not only rapidly learn new information, but to adapt the knowledge you have today to apply it in new and novel situations.*

Because we will be living a 100-year life in the future, people will be more likely to take breaks in their life away from work both to retool and to refresh. We see this happening today, with many people taking sabbaticals from work and using this time to consider exploring new options in their life. The future will be less about one career and more about a portfolio of experiences that make up a career. In Figure 5.1, we illustrate the change in the arc of our lives and how we will spend our time.

Figure 5.1 The Changing Arc of Life

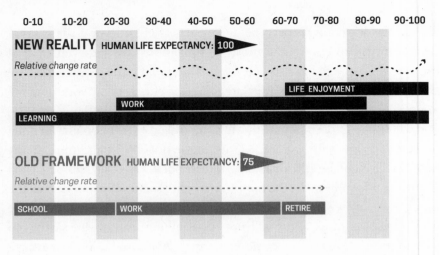

According to Deloitte's 2016 *Global Human Capital Trends* study, more than 8 out of 10 global managers view learning as an "important" or "very important issue" for organizations. People of all ages need to continuously reskill and upskill to remain relevant in today's business environment. However, companies are realizing that they cannot keep up with the demand for personalized, dynamic, continuous learning opportunities. As a result, they are shifting to self-directed practices that enable people to develop themselves (e.g., on-the-job learning opportunities, access to MOOCs or other online content that has been curated for their experience, or the building of corporate "universities" that curate multimedia learning paths).

WHAT IT MEANS TO BE A GROWTH MINDSET ORGANIZATION

Dr. Carol Dweck from Stanford University has introduced research regarding two mindsets and how they impact the way people approach their lives and work. She calls them the "fixed mindset" and the "growth mindset."[9] Dweck's research interest in this area began with her fascination for the different reactions that children have when faced with a difficult problem to solve. Some children became very anxious, while others got excited about the opportunities difficult problems posed for them. Her research concluded that some people are raised with the idea that they are born with a *fixed* level of intelligence. Others are raised to believe that through persistence and hard work, intelligence can be *grown*.

Her work argues that many managers and companies emphasize the fixed mindset. Employees are selected and compensated for their inherent brilliance or talent. You hire the "A" player because they are smart. This mindset views talent as static. But employees with a fixed mindset avoid challenges and obstacles because less-than-stellar performance might cause others to question their initial assumptions about their brilliance. These employees exert minimal effort because things should come easily to them and exerting more effort will not change the result—you either have it or you don't. Fixed mindset employees ignore negative feedback because they have been told they are better than others, so why should others' opinions matter? Interestingly, fixed mindset employees are threatened by others' success because it endangers their relative standing in the world. They should be the only ones with outstanding performance because they are the best.

In contrast, people with a growth mindset embrace challenge and work hard when faced with obstacles, because they see these situations as a path to personal growth. Growth mindset individuals seek out and embrace all types of feedback as a point of learning. They are inspired by the success from others and seek other people out to try to learn from them. For people with a growth mindset, it's exciting to take on a new challenge or learn something new.

To become a learning organization, a company needs to foster a growth mindset. A company's leaders must promote, in word and deed, the idea that if given the chance, everyone can learn new skills. Leaders must weigh their words in thinking about how their organization will be perceived. Companies that say things such as "We hire superstars" indicate a mindset of selecting people for inherent fixed traits. Companies that state their belief in hiring curious, motivated people who are willing to work hard and grow professionally exhibit a growth mindset. This mindset is also demonstrated by encouraging all employees, at all levels of the organization, to learn and grow. Just because you are a vice president does not mean you can no longer learn. In today's world, we all need to keep learning.

> *"The term [learning organization] at its core describes an organization that values and enables learning, and it becomes part of the reason to join and stay. Learning becomes part of how you get work done and how to solve problems."*
> —Karen May, former vice president, People Development, Google

EVOLVING FROM TRAINING TO LEARNING

The old model of periodic training at career inflection points (onboarding, new manager training, etc.) is giving way to the necessity of training beyond these special moments in time. Today, learning is about helping individuals remain marketable and growing their value with the company.

Companies need to shift from traditional training methods that tend to favor formal, classroom-style training removed from the real work situation. This style of training tends to lack impact because employees are not encouraged by their manager to use what they have learned. Worse yet, the culture of the team, department or company may create resistance to attempts to engage in the new behaviors learned in training. This effectively snuffs out any learning that could have happened. But learning while doing embeds the knowledge in the learner's brain by creating meaningful connections to work activities.

According to Karen May, Google's former vice president of People Development, "If learning is something that is separate from getting work done, you have made an artificial distinction. Most learning happens in the course of work, but learning in 'real time' requires attention. This is an investment that will help accelerate your performance."[10] She makes a very important point: learning requires attention. The most effective way to learn from any experience—classroom training or an on-the-job experience—is to build in time for reflection. This may be as simple as having a manager ask, "What did you learn and how are you going to apply this in your work setting?"

At Google, People Operations sends thank-you notes to managers of program participants to thank them for their support and ask them to help their employee reflect and think about how to apply what they have learned back in the workplace. Managers are provided with a set of structured questions to ask their employees, to help employees reflect and actively think about what they will do differently. By engaging the manager in this way, a commitment to change is built that provides managers with an opportunity to come back to employees and inquire later how well they have been able to apply the learning in the context of their jobs.

In *The Expertise Economy*, Kelly Palmer and David Blake promote the idea that for companies to stay competitive they need to "encourage employees to 'own' their professional development every day."[11] The authors address the importance of leaders encouraging their employees to *personalize* their own learning experiences, both what they want to learn and how they want to learn it.

Today there are so many ways that employees can learn that do not involve classroom training. Many learning and development functions are shifting from producing content to curating the best available content to meet the organization's needs. This means providing employees with access to video, readings, online courses, blogs, conferences, peer-to-peer learning networks and on-the-job learning. When they have access to all these different types of resources, employees can choose the approach that best suits them.

Integrating Learning into the Employee Experience

Going forward, learning and development is more about gaining exposure to different experiences that build new skills. Gaining access to micro-learning opportunities—such as working on a task force or helping on a project team for a short duration—is a core tenet of the Inside Gig that will facilitate skill acquisition and career growth much more quickly than approaches used in the past. Stepping out of your job to go to formal training in a classroom is augmented by learning experiences that are integrated into the flow of work. Bite-size on-the-job learning and online learning are becoming the new normal for rapid skill development. Suggesting to an employee that they access a YouTube video (sometimes on the company's own YouTube channel) to provide specific instruction to learn a new skill, while they are in the process of executing a new task, is one new way of learning while doing. The content is specific to the task at hand and can be quickly accessed in the midst of doing the task.

"We want to have a culture of development where people can fully leverage all of their talents and we can build the capabilities we need to be competitive in the marketplace. And our Experience Marketplace will take us a long way toward this."
—Christine Landon, head of Learning & Development, eBay

CASE STUDIES: EBAY AND GOOGLE

Case Study: eBay

At eBay, what the company referred to as an Experience Marketplace was piloted to give employees an opportunity to expand their skill sets and enrich their career portfolios by engaging, with manager approval, in temporary or part-time development experiences. A variety of projects were made available to employees with the intention of offering growth opportunities outside their current positions. This enabled employees to build new skills while remaining in their current roles. It complemented the classic approach to talent mobility, which involves employees changing roles or moving to new geographies to get new experiences. The Experience Marketplace is one way to make learning part of the employee experience.

Case Study: Google

Google's g2g program (Googler to Googler) is focused on creating a forum for employees who are not part of People Operations to teach other employees. It enables their 100,000-plus employees to share their expertise and passions with colleagues in a way that encourages curiosity and knowledge sharing. While many of the courses are focused on specific work skills (sales, engineering, coding), other courses focus on personal interests or well-being (yoga, new mothers returning to work). Peer coaching and mentoring also happen under the g2g offering.

Over 10 percent of Google employees are involved in the g2g program to voluntarily make time in their day to help other Googlers to learn something new. This program does not just benefit learners. Teachers benefit by honing their presentation skills, learning more deeply by teaching others, and focusing on their own continuous improvement. Employees get feedback after delivering their courses, which helps them learn and grow. The primary reason for becoming a teacher in this program is to share a passion with others. For those interested in creating their own peer-to-peer learning program, Google's re:work website indicates the following three beliefs are key to their program's success:

- All employees have the right to learn, regardless of location, role, tenure or level in the organization.
- Learning is the responsibility of the entire company, not just the Learning & Development team.
- Trust that employees are smart, capable and motivated—they have the capacity to grow Google's learning culture.[12]

While many learning and development organizations may fear that the quality of the training offered by "untrained" employees may be poor, Google sees equivalent scores for employee trainers as they do for both their own internal training professions and external trainers they hire to teach specific programs.[13] While many of the g2g trainers simply teach what they know with little oversight other than the rating they receive after the fact, those peers who teach a harder curriculum (e.g., conflict resolution) would get certified in the content prior to being able to teach that specific course. The g2g program is a wonderful example of how organizations are making learning part of the employee experience.

THE ROLE OF CULTURE IN CONTINUOUS LEARNING

While there are many different definitions of *organizational culture*, the definition we particularly like is given by SHRM: "culture consists of shared beliefs and values established by leaders and then communicated and reinforced through various methods, ultimately shaping employee perceptions, behaviors and understanding."[14] The various methods that reinforce culture include rules, policies, training recognition and rewards systems, and symbols.

When creating a culture that supports a learning organization, it all begins with the CEO—how the CEO communicates the need to become a learning organization, what this means to the CEO, how it ties in to the values espoused by the company, and how it is integrated into the expected behaviors at all levels of the organization. Leaders at all levels must be role models for learning. They must not only support those below them for taking time to learn, but they must also be active learners.

In most companies, it is not uncommon to hear that while employees want to engage in learning activities, they are so overwhelmed by their workload that they cannot take time away from the task at hand. This, of course, is reinforced by managers who say, "It's okay for you to go to that training, as long as you get all of your work done first." A laughable comment for most. It is in these moments that the company culture must embrace learning as a valued experience. Managers must view learning as a priority and encourage employees to invest in their own future, not discourage the experience.

In a culture where learning is valued, managers are incentivized to create learning opportunities. Several organizations hold their managers accountable for fostering learning by asking employees on pulse surveys if their managers are supporting them in taking on learning opportunities or providing them with stretch opportunities. Employee growth and development must be a behavior that is built into HR systems to encourage their use.

It is not easy to change a company's culture to become a learning organization. As Figure 5.2 Culture Change Model shows, culture is defined by the norms that shape internal beliefs employees hold about how people behave. These beliefs are expressed in terms of the values a company espouses and the activities to which management pays attention. Because culture is so engrained in an organization, you can't simply move one lever to create culture change. Attention must be paid to multiple levers at once to ensure that they all reinforce the same desired behavior change. Leaders must model the desired culture. Organizational communications must consistently reinforce the same messages. Selection, development and promotions must all assess competencies that support the desired culture. Since what gets measured and rewarded gets done, the organization's reward system, structure and symbols (e.g., recognition programs) must all reinforce the desired change.

Figure 5.2 Culture Change Model

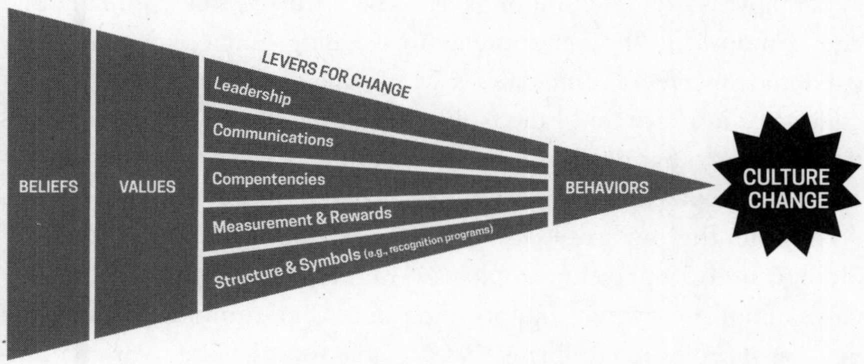

According to Palmer and Blake, a learning culture is "an environment where learning is part of everyday work, and where learning is more than compliance or required training. It is a culture where people can learn in their own time and in their own way by accessing all types of both formal and information learning including videos, articles, podcasts, books and even attending events."[15] Employees who value learning and focus on learning every day will be able to pivot and change as their work lives continue to shift and evolve.

IMPORTANCE OF LEARNING ON EMPLOYEE MOTIVATION AND RETENTION

To respond to the digital transformation that most companies are going through today, it is important to operate from a growth mindset. However, this mindset is still rare. Employers underestimate the willingness of employees to acquire the new skills required to advance into a world of automation. The Accenture Future Workforce Worker & C-Suite Surveys indicate that one in four employers believe that their employees are *resistant* to acquiring new skills. Data do not support this perception: 67 percent of workers in general, and 75 of millennial employees, believe it is important for them to develop new skills.[16] Employees do understand the importance of learning to their own career survival.

Employees are much more likely to be attracted to a company that can demonstrate its commitment to learning and opportunities for career advancement. One Sales & Marketing organization in the semiconductor industry that Edie Goldberg consulted to clearly articulated the behaviors that define success at multiple career stages and the different types of career opportunities available to entering employees. As a result, they were able to increase their offer acceptance rate from 30 percent to 75 percent. Employees want to know that their company cares about their career opportunities and opportunities to learn and grow as a professional. Firms that are able to articulate their commitment to learning will be in a better position to attract talent in this very tight labor market.

The central message of Dan Pink's book *Drive*[17] focuses on the motivation that is created when individuals have autonomy, mastery and purpose at work. *Autonomy* refers to allowing employees to be self-directed. Let's face it—the command-and-control days of management were appropriate for an earlier era. But given that most employees today are knowledge workers who are hired for what they know and what they can do, today's managers need to focus on removing roadblocks and inspiring employees—not telling them how to do their job. This is what autonomy is all about—allowing people to perform a task in the best way that they see fit.

Mastery is the desire to make progress and learn and grow, which is directly addressed when you create a learning organization. Mastery might be simply about seeing a project through to completion and learning from that process, or it might refer to gaining deeper expertise through doing the work in a different context or at a larger scale.

Purpose refers to being part of something larger. Purpose provides personal meaning for work. It is about helping employees connect what they do to a greater good (e.g., making computers available to all, which creates better equality; improving patients' health; or providing others with self-confidence to be their best).

In today's constantly evolving business environment, learning has become an important commodity for employees. Employees understand that if they are not learning, they can't advance in their careers. Therefore, several research studies have demonstrated that providing learning opportunities is a great way to retain employees and keep them from looking for the next opportunity elsewhere. LinkedIn's 2018 Learning Report indicated 93 percent of employees would stay at a company longer if it invested in their career.[18] And when employees were asked, "What would make you start to look for another job?" their top response was the inability to learn and grow with their current employer.[19] Clearly, becoming a learning organization will help companies not only to implement the Inside Gig concept in their company, but also to attract, engage and retain talent under any talent operating model.

PERSPECTIVES FROM THE INSIDE GIG

The Employee

Employees who work for learning organizations have more opportunities to enhance their current skills or build new skills to help them advance their careers. This allows them to explore new career possibilities within the company, while still benefiting from the security of their current job. If those new career options prove to be energizing, employees can build the skills they need to become successful candidates for an internal job transfer.

Learning organizations integrate learning into the flow of work so employees don't necessarily have to put in time above and beyond their day-to-day job to learn new things. Breaking work down into projects and creating bite-size learning opportunities allows employees to reskill or upskill to become more valuable to their employers. As a result, employees do not need to switch companies to gain access to career building prospects.

Not everyone learns in the same way or at the same pace. By having different types of resources to access for learning (e.g., on-the-job learning, videos, books, on-demand courses), employees can personalize their learning to formats that best suit their individual styles of learning. Personal development is a keystone of the Inside Gig, as Laura Callahan's personal story can attest.

Laura Callahan, Manager, Developer Relations, HERE Technologies

I joined HERE (at the time, NAVTEQ) in 2010 as an intern with the business affairs team. I was studying economics at DePaul University, so working on the licensing and pricing side of the company was a natural fit. It provided me with a strong, fundamental knowledge of our core business, partners and customers.

In early 2017, I relocated to the Seattle office. I was exposed to new teams, different ways of working and a side of the company I hadn't seen yet. Developer relations was one of those teams. The team's mission spoke to me and I knew I wanted to get involved, but I didn't know how or in what capacity. I contacted the developer relations program manager to learn about the team and her role, and she suggested I shadow her as a part-time program manager, using the new talent platform as the mechanism to facilitate this. I experienced not only a new team and body of work but also a type of work (program management) that I hadn't considered as a career option. Even better, I could tap into my existing network and community at HERE in my new role to accomplish things for the team.

Had it not been for the direct exposure and hands-on job experience provided through the HERE Talent Platform, I wouldn't be where I am today—with eyes open even further to new learning opportunities and next career moves waiting to be found.

The Manager

The time to market is getting shorter and shorter for companies. Hiring new employees takes time in terms of onboarding, training and getting a new employee up to speed. By providing employees with opportunities to learn either while doing their current role or by taking on a small project on another team to build new skills, managers can quickly update their teams' skills without enduring the costly delays of hiring new employees with the desired skill sets.

When managers understand how the skill sets of their employees need to evolve within their department, they can create ways for current employees to learn. They can temporarily bring in external resources to transfer skills to the team or allow employees to find on-demand resources to help build new skills. By encouraging employees to take the time to learn, managers create higher-performing teams that are able to adapt as workplace needs change. This enables managers to take control of the supply of skills within the organization.

The number one reason employees give for leaving an employer is career advancement opportunities. Often managers lose talent because they hold employees back from new opportunities because they do not want to lose their best assets. These managers put the team goals at risk by not keeping the skills on the team to execute the necessary tasks. By encouraging employees to take opportunities to learn and grow—whether that be a temporary assignment on another team, a stretch opportunity within the current department, or taking advantage of the resources offered by the company for personalized learning—managers will be able to retain talent longer. In addition, those employees will bring their newly developed skills back to the team to help improve the team's overall performance.

The Company

In today's business environment, it is imperative that organizations learn to be nimble and adaptable to changing market conditions. This is only possible by adopting a growth mindset and developing processes that encourage a constant focus on discovering new technologies, innovating the way work gets done, leveraging tools and techniques from other disciplines to do work differently, and continuously learning to maintain the most up-to-date skills. By building learning agility, a company can gain competitive advantage that will help it transform and not only survive the next business model disruption but thrive in it.

KEY TAKEAWAYS

- Given a tight labor market and constantly evolving skill sets, companies will need to invest more in upskilling and reskilling their workforces.

- With an ever-rising life expectancy, the old life model of school, work and then retirement needs to change. People are likely to have many different careers in their lifetime. Thus, they will move back and forth between learning and working overtime.

- To become learning organizations, companies need to adopt a growth mindset. They must believe that curiosity is valued and that with effort everyone can (and should) learn new skills and grow professionally, regardless of their position in the organization.

- It is critical for leaders to role-model and reinforce the importance of learning to the company's success. Managers must be held accountable for creating learning experiences for employees and for encouraging employees to take time for personal growth.

- Learning needs to evolve from classroom training at career inflection points to continuous learning while doing, supplemented by a wide variety of curated content (video, blogs, books, online learning).

- Companies that build a learning organization have a talent strategy advantage; they will be more likely to attract, engage and retain talent.

REFLECTION POINTS

Would you say that your organization has a fixed mindset or growth mindset?

Has the company's leadership put learning into place as a pro-active measure, recognizing how it will need to pivot to remain relevant to its customers?

Would you support having your direct reports invest some of their work hours to prepare for a new role or emerging skills needed in the organization?

If your company has embraced continuous learning, has its messaging changed with respect to its hiring practices to attract talent?

Do your managers support or discourage employees from taking the time to learn new skills?

Are you an active learner?

CHAPTER 6
Principle No. 4: Democratize the Work

Destiny is no matter of chance. It is not a thing to be waited for.
It's a thing to be achieved.
—William Jennings Bryan

IMAGINE THE BEGINNING OF A NEW ERA for employees and their relationships with employers. Work as we've known it is being disrupted, rethought and redesigned, and is becoming more user-friendly. Imagine that the way you think about the roles of managers and employees must change, and that the greatest challenge and opportunity for managers is to navigate from a hierarchical control orientation to adopting much more of a coach and mentor mindset.

THE FUTURE IS HERE—NOW

If you don't believe that work as we've traditionally known it is changing, here is some prevailing wisdom on the subject. In 2003, science fiction writer William Gibson was quoted in an interview for *The Economist* as saying, "The future is already here—it's just not evenly distributed." In 2018, Anna Tunkel wrote an article that appeared in *Forbes,* in which she elaborated on the future Gibson envisioned. In the next 20 years, Tunkel wrote, we should expect to see significant disruptions in the workforce, due to factors such as demographic trends, globalization, advances in technology, increasing automation of jobs and machine learning. She points out that a wide range of institutions from the World Bank to MIT have launched initiatives to study this evolution of jobs. As a result, there is an ever-expanding quest for talent development and deployment.[1]

THE JOB BLUES

How many times during your career have you felt stuck in a job? It's when you stare at the time on your smart device and time moves infinitely slowly. It's the feeling that you aren't contributing and making a difference, or it could be that boredom has set in. You may have grown out of your job, even though your job description hasn't changed in years. What may have worked in the industrial revolutions of the past no longer makes sense. Consider some of the recent research and reports about the disruptions that are occurring to the world of work.

A 2018 research study by Deloitte concluded that companies are rethinking how jobs are structured as a way of increasing the value contributions of the workforce.[2]

A recent article by Thomas Oppong notes that the work being done in organizations today has in some cases changed quite dramatically. It is evolving from routine skills common during industrialization to the emergence of more and more automation, which is replacing human workers or making some jobs obsolete.[3]

Irving Wladawsky-Berger's "Jobs Outlook for 2022" boldly states that it's essential for businesses to redefine work if they're going to remain competitive in the 21st century. The trend toward more automation, it goes on to say, creates opportunities to free up workforce capacity for higher-level skill application. This, the article claims, shifts the conversation about the future of work, which should result in a win for both individual employees and their companies.[4]

Todd Henry, author of *The Accidental Creative: How to Be Brilliant at a Moment's Notice*, has stated: "The global economy is changing, and the very definition of 'job' is changing right along with it."[5]

A World Economic Forum report notes that significant changes in job and skill demands in the Fourth Industrial Revolution are bringing with them even greater challenges to the problem of accurately matching individuals to opportunities. Indeed, the report goes on to say that the core skills required to perform most roles will, on average, change by approximately 42 percent.[6]

McKinsey & Company issued a future of work report specifically focused on the impact of automation. One conclusion from their survey suggests that existing technologies could potentially automate about half of the work people currently perform around the globe. Indeed, approximately 60 percent of all occupations, and perhaps one-third of the work performed in those occupations, could be automated. Substantial workplace transformation and disruption are clearly under way.[7]

While working on the CHREATE Project, we spent many months mapping how organizations must evolve to meet future challenges, defining and redefining work and the requisite skills for adapting to a new future. Figure 6.1, The Four Kinds of Work in the Future, illustrates the consortium's conclusions about the four major categories work will likely fall into in the future.

The four potential scenarios will evolve based on the amount of choice in the work being performed (democratization of work) and the enablement of technology to transform the way we work, enabling companies to match the work to the skills of the workforce (technological empowerment). Having choices at work will likely mean higher levels of engagement in the workforce, as workers determine where their values and interests align to the work.

 Democratization of work is a term to describe how control or choice is applied in the work environment. You can, for example, democratize the work by creating an internal marketplace of projects through which employees can choose the type of work that suits their interests and skills.

In their book *The Future-Proof Workplace*, Linda Sharkey and Morag Barrett note that employers will continue to tap in to more flexible workforces, using technology solutions to grow and shrink teams

Figure 6.1 The Four Kinds of Work in the Future
How the democratization and technological empowerment of work will affect organizations.

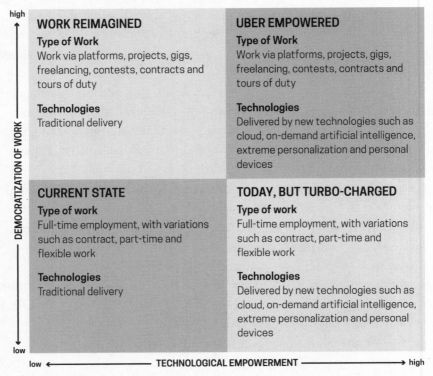

Source: John Boudreau, "Work in the Future Will Fall into These Four Categories," *Harvard Business Review*, March 17, 2016. © HBR.org, using CHREATE data, 2015.

quickly. They make it clear that, in the future, employees will expect to fit work around their personal lives rather than fitting their lives around work.[8]

So, if you are experiencing the job blues, it's clear that the nature of work and jobs is changing, in some cases faster than anticipated. This presents companies with enormous challenges as well as with potential opportunities. Some obvious challenges include a need for new ways to structure work; for revised incentive systems to attract and reward employees; for new ways of thinking about performance, teams, collaboration and culture; and perhaps most important, for a significant mindset shift to enable adoption of these new ways of working. Competitive opportunities include a chance to unleash the vast, untapped potential of employees; a shift from restrictive job-description-based accountabilities to more robust measurements of value-added contributions; and, of course, a path to elevating talent assets on the balance sheet along with capital asset valuations.

DEMOGRAPHIC DRIVERS AND WORKFORCE PROJECTIONS

An important dynamic of the gig economy is affected by demographics in the workplace. You may ask: What is really driving an interest in allowing for more choice at work, and is choice tied to generations or age groups? And how do we distinguish and categorize these workforces? Depending on the source, researchers report similarities in the age cutoffs used to differentiate various generations. As of 2019, a commonly used breakdown by age looked like this:

- *Baby boomers*, born between 1946 and 1964, are currently between 55 and 73 years old (there are 72 million in the U.S.).

- *Gen X*, born between 1965 and 1980, are currently between 39 and 54 years old (82 million in the U.S.).

- *Gen Y*, or *millennials*, born between 1981 and 1996, are currently between 23 and 38 years old (73 million in the U.S.).

- *Gen Z*, the newest generation to be named, were born between 1997 and the present; they are currently between 0 and 22 years old (nearly 74 million in the U.S.).[9]

Workforce projections for the coming decades highlight a number of noteworthy developments. Patricia Buckley and Daniel Bachman, in their article for the *Deloitte Review* called "Meet the U.S. Workforce of the Future," point out that despite projections that workforce participation from the over-55 age group will continue to modestly rise by

2024, millennials will represent the largest share of any single genera-tion.[10] Thus the often anxious discussions about the millennial generation and their seemingly unconventional motivations and work preferences. Simply stated, millennials are redefining work.

Interestingly, descriptions of millennials by many lay observers include blanket generalizations such as "They display a notable urgency to make social change" or "They seem to have an altruistic commit-ment." Millennials have also been pegged, not very flatteringly, as "narcissistic praise hounds" whose goal is "wealth and fame."[11]

However, research tells us something different. Two independent studies investigating differences between generations in terms of values and motivations found surprising results. The first, published in the *Journal of Management*, studied generational differences. The authors note that when comparing various data points, one conclusion is that the generations are quite similar. On average, all generations studied rated what are called intrinsic values (interesting work, being chal-lenged and learning opportunities) the highest; followed by extrinsic values (pay, promotions, status and helping others) in the middle; and leisure and social rewards (vacation time, work-life balance and social interactions) at the bottom. The researchers' surprising conclusion was that *age* rather than one's generation is what determines values and motivations.[12]

In the second study, psychologist Jennifer Deal elegantly describes in *Retiring the Generation Gap* that "all generations have similar values; they just express them differently. We might have unique ways of getting there, but we pretty much want the same things out of work."[13]

In a 2018 Gallup study, one of the conclusions was something psy-chologists have known for decades: all workers have basic psychological needs that must be met in order to perform at high levels of motivation. So despite the complexities surrounding new forms of working rela-tionships, the report goes on to say that gig workers are just like every-one else—motivated and inspired much like most other, more traditional workers with perhaps only a few distinctions.[14]

In *Bury My Heart in Conference Room B*, Stan Slap describes a series of interviews where he asked employees what they wanted in their jobs.

Their responses included statements such as "wanting to have an impact," "wanting to make a difference" and "wanting to live their personal values at work."[15] It's clear that no matter what generation or age group, there is an intrinsic need to get up every day and make a difference in your work life as well as your personal life. It is clear that the power to choose work that has intrinsic value is key to motivation and engagement.

CHANGING THE WAY WE THINK ABOUT WORK

Work is being redesigned to create maximum benefit to all stakeholders and value for a company. The term *value* in this context does not simply mean cost-cutting measures or operational efficiencies. In a 2018 Deloitte Insights article on redefining work, the authors note:

> Employers can begin to redefine work and expand value by considering three shifts:
>
> 1. Shifting the view of the objective of work from efficiencies to expanding the value delivered to customers and other stakeholders.
> 2. Fundamentally redefining work from executing routine tasks to addressing unseen problems and opportunities.
> 3. Cultivating and using our human qualities from skills-based work to capabilities-based work.[16]

 Capabilities-based work *refers to work that is focused on the potential of individuals to perform certain tasks based on their skills or capabilities.*

An article by Edelman research suggests that to succeed in running a business in the gig economy, companies must learn to break down large-scale projects into short-term actions and tasks. Work must be envisioned in the same way that technology companies organize product development release cycles rather than according to delivery of the end product. Teams can then focus more directly on the tasks in front of them and use those results to inform the next step in the process. This will also enable more direct and immediate feedback along the way.[17]

Noted business school professors and strategy gurus Gary Hamel and C.K. Prahalad stated some years ago: "The traditional resource allocation task of top management has received too much attention when compared to the task of resource leverage. Instead of achieving linear growth by adding new resources, companies should more efficiently extract the capability of people and watch growth skyrocket."[18]

THE POWER OF CHOICE

One defining characteristic of the post–baby boomer generations of workers is their strong desire to have more choice about the work they do. One study notes that while millennials don't expect something for nothing, they do believe that if they demonstrate responsibility, they should have a commensurate degree of autonomy. Other surveys highlight priorities for the millennial generation as being a desire to work for the greater good along with the desire to do something big.

In a *Psychology Today* article about having choices, the author notes that "an abundance of choice in our everyday lives is regarded as a luxury of modern living. The option to choose is something that we no longer just value but now *expect*—it is a prerequisite that people are given the option to *choose* between two or more ideas."[19]

In her study "What Millennials Really Want at Work," Anna Bahney found that the millennial generation seems to value experiences over money. The participants ranked "being in jobs they are passionate about" higher than salary in importance. Indeed, when asked what they valued most in a job, the response they gave more often than any other was "freedom."[20] Merriam-Webster's dictionary defines *freedom* as "the absence of . . . constraint in choice." Regardless of one's definition of the term, the notion of democratizing work must include choice for employees.[21]

That said, research into the psychology of choice is fascinating but also a bit perplexing. As a nonscientific inquiry, if you asked people their preference between choosing from a list of five different items or a list of only two, most people would probably say that they prefer five choices. Intuitively, people feel that the more options they have, the greater their chances of finding the choice that will perfectly satisfy their needs. However, it turns out that this intuitive assumption is somewhat of an illusion.

As Sheena Iyengar, a renowned expert on the psychology of choice, notes in *The Art of Choosing*, the more choices we have, the less likely we actually are to make a decision.[22] Why, you might ask. Based on her research, Iyengar says it is because having too many options causes a sort of paralysis in the decision-making process, which leads to avoidance behavior—that is, choosing to do nothing at all. In short, when we're presented with too many options, we often fear making the wrong decision.

Researcher Liraz Margalit articulates it this way:

Human cognitive ability cannot efficiently compare more than five options, so most of us will start looking at the first few options and then stop. Awareness that there may be a better option triggers the urge to find it. However, due to time constraints and human cognitive limitations, we are unable to engage in the elaborate thought process required to compare and contrast all of the available alternatives.[23]

Regarding millennials (and indeed, any generation of workers) and the need to democratize work, both common instincts and research tell us one important thing with respect to providing more choice. Organizations need to carefully consider precisely how much freedom of choice creates the desired outcomes for all stakeholders. A delicate balancing act, indeed!

A WORKFORCE OF CONSUMERS

Younger generations view work differently than older generations. As Brandon Rigoni and Amy Adkins note in their 2016 article, "What Millennials Want from a New Job," millennials' eager willingness to switch jobs and companies presents an opportunity for employers in need of talent. Ultimately, millennials, like the rest of us, are consumers of the places in which they work. Perhaps more than other generations, they shop around for jobs and companies that best align with their needs and life goals. This suggests that employers need to focus more attention on what makes their companies attractive to this kind of consumer. They must find ways to attract potential employees and encourage potential employees to make them the employer of choice.[24]

The authors enumerate the characteristics of this new workforce. Workers are educated, know their options, and want to get more from work than just doing the job. They're hungry for experience, much like customers are hungry for experience when they purchase a product or service. As such, they should be considered another kind of customer, and as it turns out, a very difficult one to satisfy.[25] Today's consumers want their preferences, tastes and choices to be remembered by companies and websites alike.

In her book *The Gig Is Up*, Olga Mizrahi notes that today's workers have a computer in their pocket; they are "digitally enabled" consumers.[26] The employee as consumer of a total, satisfying work experience has arrived.

THE ROLE OF TECHNOLOGY IN DEMOCRATIZING WORK

It's clear that democratizing work will be a key element of how organizations compete in the future. Future-of-work expert John Boudreau identifies considerations for democratizing work including adopting the right mindset, treating employees as consumers, factoring in generational differences, and balancing employees' desire for freedom of choice with the organization's need for order and structure. He goes on to suggest that, in the future, business leaders might be able to find the required talent by literally "deconstructing work" through smart HR systems. This means identifying what tasks and skills are required to do the work, how many people it would take, and matching the right talent with the appropriate task.[27]

In the World Economic Forum report "Skills as the Currency of the Labor Market," the authors highlight how important it is for companies to shift to skills-based systems of talent sourcing, matching and deployment. They describe current methods as imperfect and perhaps even resulting in financial and non-financial losses to companies and employees. The increasing automation of work will demand that companies find innovative solutions to the intelligent management of talent resources. And workers must continuously re-evaluate and update their skill sets in order to remain relevant.[28]

Matching People to Job Requirements

As companies move to more project-based work, success will depend on the capability to accurately and rapidly match employee skill sets to required tasks. This is precisely where technology can become the great enabler. Technology offers the capability to collect, categorize, search and match employee profiles with project work. Research has long demonstrated the power of matching people skills to work requirements and its results regarding performance, job satisfaction and turnover.[29]

By adapting concepts learned from job-person fit studies, combined with technology's accelerated and comprehensive capability, the potential to usher in the future of work is no longer a remote possibility. Imagine the real-time ability to identify project requirements, then almost instantaneously find any number of employees with the exact skill sets needed for that work? Think of the implications: cycle time reductions, product quality improvements, accelerated time to market, customer experience enhancements, high-performance teams.

Consider how professional football and basketball teams operate. At game time, coaches are constantly deploying and redeploying talent, moving players in and out of situations to match the best talent available on the bench against immediate and anticipated challenges presented on the field or the court. They evaluate the situations, then look for the best available "match-ups." They ask themselves, "In this particular set of circumstances, who and where is the best talent I have available to meet the demands of this set of circumstances?" And they do it very quickly—or run the risk of losing.

The sports metaphor illustrates the required mindset: the ability to quickly match talent to circumstances. The basic requirement for developing a rapid deployment capability is to harness the correct data and get it into the hands of decision makers as quickly as possible. This is the promise technology holds for the democratization of work.

It is not only possible to "democratize the work," it's essential. If companies are to continue on the paths of innovation, competitive differentiation and best-place-to-work cultures, they must redefine work as well as the rules of working. They must let go of limiting visions and embrace the possibilities of what might be. Employees must be clear about their values, passions and desires to contribute. They must also be willing to work in unconventional ways, perhaps ways that have not yet been created. Together, they must discover where organizational visions and personal aspirations overlap, for this is where the possibility of unleashing their untapped potential awaits. The future of work is here—*now!*

CASE STUDY: DOLBY LABORATORIES

Dolby Laboratories wanted to move from strictly focusing on roles to understanding skill sets so that employees could flow through the organization and use their skills diversely and for the highest purpose possible. Dolby knew the organization had a lot of talent, and it wanted to make sure that talent was optimally deployed. But the company did not have a system that identified its employees' skills and experiences (it only had job titles and job descriptions), so it sought a solution to help it manage talent more resourcefully.

Dolby implemented a new talent platform, Hitch, which helped to develop both a skills inventory for its talent and a way to break projects down to the skills required to execute each project's components. According to George Hudgens, senior director of HR Operations, "We wanted employees to feel they could have dynamic careers at Dolby. They can move around and leverage their skills."

While the system Dolby uses matches people to available part-time opportunities, it is noteworthy that employees proactively search the listings for opportunities that might be of interest to them. Even if, due to time constraints, they are not looking for an immediate opportunity, employees like being able to see opportunities that might be a match for them or help them develop a skill they want to grow.

PERSPECTIVES FROM THE INSIDE GIG

The Employee

Without question, it's the beginning of a new era for employees and their relationships with employers. Work as we've known it is being disrupted, rethought and redesigned, and it is becoming more user-friendly. The values and motivations the emerging workforce bring to the workplace are fundamentally reshaping the nature of work itself. Employees want to do things that matter, that have purpose, that are bigger than themselves. To fulfill those aspirations, they want more choice regarding exactly what they will work on and how it connects to their values and motivations for living their lives. They are becoming the ultimate consumers of everything; companies need to pay attention and "democratize the work," or the talent shortages we so often hear about will become a symptom of dying industries.

The Manager

The industrial revolutions of the past that reshaped work and the roles of managers in the resulting economies are fading from relevance. The implication for managers now and in the future, in the poignant words of CEO coach Marshall Goldsmith: "What got you here won't get you there!" Said another way, the way we think about the roles of managers and employees must change. The mindsets of the past are no longer useful or even appropriate in the Fourth Industrial Revolution that is under way. The greatest challenge for managers will be to navigate from a hierarchical control orientation to adopting more of a coach and mentor mindset. The manager's role is to provide the guidance necessary for employees to unleash their untapped potential. This cannot be accomplished by old methods and will likely require some trial and error. The upside for managers, however, is that the possibility of enabling self-directed individual contributors and teams will exponentially increase the contributions of the workforce.

The Company

Democratizing work is at the heart of the Inside Gig concept. The freedom it offers to employees is powerful, and yes, it does mean that an organization has to think of new ways to structure work, incentivize employees and measure results. It will require a culture shift, where learning is continuous and optimism is palpable because of the possibilities that open up to elevate people and see the results of untapped talent come to fruition. The bottom line for the company is increased employee engagement, productivity and innovation.

KEY TAKEAWAYS

- The world of work is rapidly changing, and companies are trying hard to keep up. Automation, as well as the values and motivations of the younger generations, are creating the need to 1) redefine work, 2) identify who can do the work, and 3) determine where it can be done on a global ecosystem. This requires a shift in thinking about the unspoken contract between organizations and the workforce.

- Companies need to move away from simply checking the boxes of performance goals to identify the real value of the work that is being done. They need to ask, "How do we create maximum benefit to our multiple stakeholder groups—customers, employees and shareholders—and the markets in which we operate?"

• Employers must incorporate more personalized work experiences for employees. In addition, they must provide more choices for employees to do the work that truly motivates them. Employees should be thought of as consumers—consumers of a total work experience—and therefore, the work must be redefined.

• Technology plays a pivotal role not only in redefining work, but also in enabling a richer set of experiences for employees. The ability of employees to have more decision-making rights to pursue work they're passionate about can result in significant contributions to company operations. Technology will increase the ability to accurately and quickly match work requirements with available employee talent.

REFLECTION POINTS

Your workplace likely has multigenerational teams. What insights from this chapter will help you better understand team dynamics and what drives them?

Would you assess your workplace as one that offers choice to employees regarding what work they do?

Are there obvious signs in your organization that work needs to be redesigned? These signs could include employee fatigue, absenteeism, falling productivity or the introduction of new technologies.

Does your organization live its values and understand the connection to motivation and retention of staff? Would your company see the democratization of work as a challenge or an opportunity?

CHAPTER 7
Principle No. 5: Create an Agile Organization

Intelligence is the ability to adapt to change.
—Stephen Hawking

IMAGINE A WORKPLACE—YOUR WORKPLACE—where a junior employee who has the right skill set can take a project lead. A manager can access talent from anywhere across the organization to create a rapid response team. And the organizational structure is able to react quickly to changing business dynamics and gain a competitive advantage. Teams are empowered to make decisions; they are fluid in their makeup and are integral to the organization's overall responsiveness, which in turn improves customer satisfaction and loyalty. Principle No. 5, "Create an agile organization," focuses on transformation and rethinking the traditional models that have governed the way we work but are now due for a makeover.

INTRODUCING ORGANIZATION MODELS FOR THE FOURTH INDUSTRIAL REVOLUTION

The impact of the Fourth Industrial Revolution is causing companies in every industry, large and small, to consider how to take advantage of the new technologies that are becoming available to innovate, rethink and fundamentally reimagine their approach to business. Coupled with improving productivity is a desire to improve the customer experience or be more responsive to changing customer needs.

It is hard to read a business article today that does not focus on an organization's digital transformation. Digital technologies facilitate collaboration and communication across an organization; they enable people across geographies—and even across organizational boundaries—to work together. A 2018 McKinsey Global Survey found that in the past five years, more than 8 out of 10 organizations have engaged in some level of digital transformation.[1] George Westerman, principal research scientist with the MIT Sloan Initiative on the Digital Economy, argues that while digital transformation requires organizations to radically rethink how they utilize technology, what organizations must do is create a new business strategy enabled by digital technologies.[2] His research suggests that the real value in digital transformation comes from innovating people and business processes and that these process innovations lead to the true transformation of the business.

The Inside Gig is one approach to innovating people processes that helps organizations optimize the use of the talent they already have within the organization. It also provides a vehicle for continuous learning for employees as they are exposed to new technologies, new ways of approaching problems and different parts of the organization. Exposure to diverse and novel experiences leads to personal growth. If people have a variety of experiences in different areas rather than focusing all their time on routine tasks and working with the same team, they become more agile. And given the rapid transformation of organizations today, the need to become more agile as both individuals and an organization is clear.

THE NEED FOR AGILITY IN THE FACE OF CHANGE

According to Deloitte's *Global Human Capital Trends 2016* study,[3] the top trend facing organizations is an organizational redesign to shift the traditional functional models to interconnected, flexible teams that can be more agile and customer-focused. This is a significant shift from the functional or departmental silos in which businesses have operated over the past several decades.

In an era of predictability, organizations were constructed around models of efficiency. Efficiency was gained through specialization and clear delineations of who performs what type of work and how much time it took to complete. Not only were jobs well defined, but individuals were organized into functional specialties to ensure that people focusing on similar types of work worked closely together and could learn from one another and share information as appropriate. These tight-knit functions created strong networks that discouraged cross-boundary collaboration.

Contrast that era with today's unpredictability and constant business model disruption. Organizations have no choice but to be more responsive to changing business priorities and evolving customer demands. Silos within organizations remain a barrier to an organization's ability to shift gears quickly when business conditions demand it. Organization models must be built on agility and optimize the speed with which the organization can respond to change.

The principles behind organization agility have been around for decades. The underlying premise is to empower and motivate teams by giving them purpose and autonomy, to embed learning within the project, to encourage collaboration with the customer and across disciplines, and to use sprints to iterate toward a solution. Once the team has reached a solution, it disbands, and members then form new teams to solve a different problem. Lessons learned from agile software are now being applied to all facets of work.

Harvard Business Review certainly thinks that becoming more agile is the path to organizational nirvana. In its March–April 2018 issue, HBR devoted an entire section to "The New Rules of Talent Management." These articles focus on how Human Resources is adopting principles derived from Agile Software Development to advance the idea that organizations need to learn to co-create employee experiences with end users, and test and iterate on processes rather than take a year to design "the" way to do (name your HR process) and then push the one-size-fits-all process onto the entire organization. The articles present ideas on how organizations can benefit from reorganizing talent in new ways to optimize the use of their human resources. While this was an impressive dedication to the topic of Agile in HR, HBR followed up with a May–June 2018 issue titled "Agile at Scale: How to Create a Truly Flexible Organization." Clearly, becoming more agile is a topic receiving a great deal of interest.

THE RISE OF ADAPTIVE TEAM STRUCTURES

A much-discussed part of designing for agility is a shift away from traditional hierarchical structures toward organization designs that leverage dynamic teams that form and disband as needed. Each team is composed of individuals who among them have all the skills necessary to have a successful outcome, regardless of where those individuals sit organizationally. Let's face it: work is more complex than it has ever been. This complexity often requires expertise from different disciplines to solve those problems.

Both Hollywood filmmakers and most consulting firms operate in an industry that heavily relies on similar types of fluid team structures. When a new project comes up, an interdisciplinary team is formed to meet the needs of the project. When the project is completed, those individuals disband and go to work on other projects. In a consulting firm, while the functional lines of business (Strategy, Sales & Marketing, Human Capital) may be run by the firm's leadership, most of the talent in each line of business works on a set of revolving projects. Consultants provide their expertise where needed and then move on to the next project. The line-of-business leadership team manages the flow of talent from one project to the next, makes decisions on building or acquiring new capabilities and determines the future direction of that business.

"An agile organization (designed for both stability and dynamism) is a network of teams within a people-centered culture that operates in rapid learning and fast decision cycles which are enabled by technology, and that is guided by a powerful common purpose to co-create value for all stakeholders."
—Wouter Aghina et al., The Five Trademarks of Agile Organizations

Project-Based Team Structures

Just because we are suggesting to move away from a strict reliance on *structural* hierarchy does not necessarily mean that you completely do away with job titles or remove levels within the organization. An internal job title is usually tied to a job level. Job levels convey the amount of experience and expertise the individual demonstrates in their profession, as well as the amount of responsibility the position carries, in terms of either budget or direct reports.

However, research in social network analysis has demonstrated that structural level indicators are a poor gauge of actual levels of influence within the organization. The informal networks that form within organizations represent the true internal power structure. Thus, a reliance on hierarchical structure alone for decision-making is detrimental to the organization. Indeed, it can lead to unnecessary workarounds when leaders are unavailable or block a team's progress. In today's complex business operations, the abilities to build networks, enhance communication skills and influence outcomes are rapidly becoming high-demand skills that will be tied to how a role is compensated. Individuals who can master an organization's social network can advance their causes much more quickly and with greater success than individuals who do not excel in these areas.

It is often the case that the real day-to-day work is being done in teams that serve a specific purpose or need. While many thought leaders today paint a vision of a future of teams comprised primarily of people outside of your organization (freelancers, talent on demand, the external gig economy), we don't think this will be as widespread a phenomenon as many are currently predicting.

There is a great deal of value in the shared values and culture that hold teams in a company together. When Edie Goldberg worked as a thought leader in the Human Capital Practice for Towers Perrin, a global management consulting firm, she frequently worked with colleagues all over the world. She could show up anywhere, meet her colleagues for the first time, and five minutes later walk into a client's office as a united team. This was because of the common set of tools they worked with, the common frameworks they had for how to approach an assignment, and a shared culture that created norms for working together. This is how teams can form and disband without losing efficiency. However, if organizations constantly put together teams that are transient in nature, these norms and common frameworks will not exist, and the variety of perspectives team members bring will make the work much more difficult to coordinate.

Thus, the Inside Gig is a strategy that has more viability long-term than an organization winnowing down to a small core of employees and employing freelance talent to carry out the majority of the work. There will always be value in the specific skills an expert contractor brings to an organization, but companies must develop better processes to transfer that expertise to their own employees by creating an environment of learning while doing.

For multiple teams to work together effectively, each team must have clearly defined project objectives that can be shared not only within the team, but also with other teams. That way, the teams understand each other's remits.

A common example of teams that operate in this manner are product development teams in a biotechnology company. When developing a molecule into a potential treatment for a disease, biotech companies bring together individuals from a variety of disciplines (Research, Clinical, Commercial, Med Affairs, Finance, Regulatory, and so on) to create a robust process to bring a potential drug to the marketplace. The team will either be successful in bringing the drug to market or the research will not pass the hurdles needed for regulatory approval.

Either way, the team will disband and then reform in different configurations to tackle a new set of objectives.

While they work on these product development teams, individuals remain as part of their functional organization and still maintain some of the responsibilities of their "main" job description. However, in this situation the organization has found a way to make an individual's job more flexible so that time can be devoted to another team—outside of their function—to complete work that is mission-critical for the company. The same basic premise happens when developing a new product in technology companies. This is the type of organizational flexibility that we are building for the Inside Gig.

CONNECTING STREAMS OF WORK: THE SHIFT IN HIERARCHY

Hierarchies have been useful because they can help facilitate a flow of information. When you operate in a team-based structure, information does not naturally cascade in any particular manner. So it is critical to build in an infrastructure of both positions and technology that helps to facilitate the sharing of information within and across teams. Various new social technology tools are being used today to help create open and free-flowing information. But we can also learn lessons from organizations that have operated with many project teams, such as is the case in technology firms. It is helpful to have a Project Management Organization (PMO) to ensure that teams working on supportive or complementary processes connect at the right times and share information as appropriate. We all suffer from information overload today, so it's helpful to have a small team of people who can help move information to the right channels and protect people from getting information they don't need.

The Project Management Organization facilitates the organization's agility by connecting streams of work that should be informed by each other or encouraging teams to come together when their work overlaps. Project teams can be amoeba-like structures that expand and contract as the needs of the project dictate. While most teams will have a common core, there may be some expertise that the teams need to rely on only for a short period or at a particular point in the project. There is no need for someone to sit on a project for the duration, when their expertise is not being fully utilized. So, another form of agility is thinking about teams as organisms that change over time; they do not always need to be the same (as a department team would).

The people who are chosen to lead teams are not assumed to be in charge because they are in a position of leadership. Instead, project team leaders are individuals with the knowledge, skills and expertise needed to make the team successful, and who have the project leadership skills to bring a team together for success. In this way, leadership is earned, not appointed. This example may help clarify our point. For a project redesigning one process, Leader A may be the best person to lead the team, but for another project team, Leader A's expertise is only be needed to a smaller extent. Their role is more appropriately a team contributor rather than a team leader. The structure of the team fits the purpose for that team. It is also possible for leadership to shift as the team goes through different phases of the project, letting the subject matter expert lead when appropriate.

Let's look at what we mean about moving from hierarchies to networks of teams from a graphic point of view.

Figure 7.1 Hierarchy of Today shows an example of how organizations are typically designed today. There is one leader at the top (the CEO), and then a line of direct reports to the leader (function or department heads). Below this will be a series of sub-team leads with more employees.

However, in Figure 7.2 Networks of Teams, not only is the team lead not pictured in a hierarchical manner, but we begin to see the social network that ties people together across the teams. In this case, the woman in the bottom left of the diagram appears to have many connections across all the teams. While she may or may not be the leader for her project team, the value she brings to the organization should be recognized: she has the ability to connect ideas across projects. The loss of this talent to the organization would be more detrimental than that of someone who is not as well connected.

Figure 7.1 Hierarchy of Today

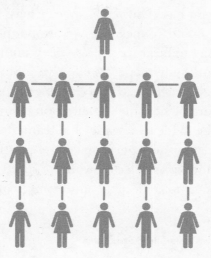

Figure 7.2 Networks of Teams

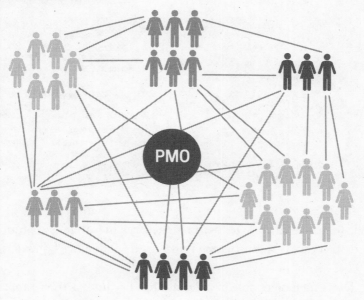

Table 7.1 Hierarchies vs. Team-Based Structures summarizes the key differences between operating under a traditional hierarchy and operating in a team-based structure. We believe that the future is about collaboration and connection. We are not proposing the complete demise of hierarchical structures. They are necessary to make a project-based work system operate effectively. But we are suggesting that the team-based structures overlay the hierarchical structures and influence the culture of how the organization operates. Big organization bets will still be made by a leadership team that is focused on the organization's strategy and performance. But strict reliance on a hierarchical structure is out of step with the speed of business today, and it certainly does not reflect the autonomy that employees desire in their work.

Table 7.1 Hierarchies vs. Team-Based Structures

Hierarchies	Team-Based Structures
Leaders have position-based authority	Leaders are selected because they are experts in their domain
Focus is on title	Focus is on contribution
Structure provides control	Structure is designed for adaptability
Intent of organization design is to create predictability	Organization is designed for emergence
Decision-making is centralized	Teams are empowered to make decisions locally
Information is cascaded down the organization	Social technologies are adopted to create a rapid flow of information to all those impacted
Poor communication at lower levels of the organization	Strong communication at all levels of the organization

So, to move from a focus on structural hierarchies to more team-based structures, begin by engaging in the following behaviors:

1. Don't include people in meetings just because of their rank. Include them because they need to be part of the dialogue to do the work.

2. Push decision-making down to the team level to empower the teams to act quickly.

3. Ensure you have collaboration tools in place to facilitate the free flow of information within and between related teams.

4. Ensure proper team development gets established at the outset. In particular, set clear goals for the team to unite them around a common mission.

5. Invite people to be on your team because of what they can contribute to the team. If you need expertise from elsewhere in the organization, invite that individual to be present.

6. Manage the work, not the political structure.

After the 2008 financial crisis, many organizations removed layers of management simply to survive, so organizational hierarchies became flattened. For the past decade, organizations have been transitioning to figure out how to work optimally in this new, flatter structure. The flattening of hierarchical structures has had a consequential impact on career promotions. It has made the roles at successively higher levels monumentally larger roles. It was once easy to "climb the rungs of the corporate ladder" because the rungs were close to one another. Now, that ladder is broken, because the rungs are too far apart. Career promotions require not just more experience in the same area, but a breadth of experiences to manage a broader group of individuals. So employees need to focus more on building experiences than on simply taking the next step up an invisible corporate ladder—now you need to navigate a jungle gym of experiences to progress in a career. There's been a movement from career promotion to career progression.

Traditional organizational structures have only been around for about a century. While they have served us well, it is now time to reconsider each company's organization design and whether it is serving the needs of the business. Is there an opportunity to rethink how your company is organized? Could it be nimbler and take advantage of a more flexible structure to address new projects, issues or opportunities with more agility as they arise? Do you need to stop talking about career promotion (which relies on hierarchical structures), and speak more about career progression (which helps employees build the mosaic that will ultimately complete the picture of their life)? Is it time to focus less on structure and more on experiences and capability building?

The Inside Gig will enable this type of cross-boundary collaboration. It places these opportunities on a talent platform so that companies can access talent from across the organization, whether they are in a different geography or a different function. Being able to easily form the team you need, when you need it, is the advantage a talent platform brings to any business. Talent platforms search explicitly for skills and experiences and do not look at job titles. Chapter 9, A New Talent Operating Model: Rethinking Ways of Working, will address issues around culture that will support this new agile approach to work.

Despite the advantages to working in dynamic team structures, it won't be practical to make a wholesale move to these types of structures because baby boomers will resist. They want both the title and the recognition as they move up in the organizational hierarchy. But business leaders need to start thinking in this direction and building in more agility for people to work on projects in teams to meet business needs and then disband and work on other things—just like they do in consulting firms and in Hollywood.

RETHINKING THE MANAGER ROLE

If organizational structures are moving from a focus on structures based on function to more team-based structures, what happens to the role of the manager? This is an interesting question if you are a manager, but if you consider instead that you are a leader, there is a place to ask whether this is an *important* question. If you focus on doing the work as most managers do today, you will find out that most managers today don't spend much of their time managing people. Most managers spend their time leading projects. As such, many have argued for years that we need to redefine the role of the manager.

That said, in parts of the organization the traditional manager and employee relationship may still structurally make the most sense, given the work that is being completed by that group and how it is being completed (e.g., independent tasks, routine work). However, in other parts of the organization, where project-based work is more the norm, it's worth asking if this is the right structure moving forward. Thus, we suggest you use the structure that makes the most sense for the work being performed. This is ultimately a judgment call.

In a project-based environment (where the Inside Gig is the vehicle for distributing work equitably among employees), the traditional role of "manager" does not make as much sense. The skills that a manager needs are less about organizing and distributing work to their group and more about providing coaching and guidance to employees. Since this is probably the task that most managers are least skilled in and like doing the least, let's redefine this position and make sure it is given, like everything else in the project-based world, to people with the skills and interests to excel in the task.

In a project-based environment, we recommend that in lieu of a manager, companies adopt a career coach role that complements the project leader role. Project leaders lead the work that is to be accomplished. A career coach should be a management-level individual from the appropriate functional area of expertise that can serve as a mentor and coach to the employee; they should be senior enough to share wisdom. The career coach acts as an advocate for their employees. This person helps to gather and synthesize performance information across multiple systems to help employees make sense of the input and use it to inform their own personal development plans.

In addition to other leadership responsibilities they hold, career coaches would spend a greater percentage of their time coaching and mentoring a larger number of individuals within their discipline. Unlike the former manager role, which was 90 percent individual contributor activities and 10 percent manager activities, these individuals will be selected for their expertise in coaching and mentoring, and will thus spend a greater proportion of their time engaged in those activities. These individuals will be invested in ensuring their coachees are focused on the right activities to develop their skills and advance their careers.

One measure of the success of a career coach will be the retention and advancement of the employees they serve. To best support their role, they will also be highly engaged in the strategic planning and direction of the function, so they understand what capabilities the organization needs to build and what capabilities are no longer core to the business. Table 7.2 Roles and Responsibilities Defined differentiates the traditional responsibilities of the manager role with the new expectations for a project leader (which will be transient from project to project) and a career coach.

Table 7.2 Roles and Responsibilities Defined

Manager (old)	Project Leader	Career Coach (new)
• Provides team with context for their work • Distributes responsibilities across team members based on their role, skills and capacity • Provides oversight and direction to direct reports • Addresses performance issues • Completes administrative duties	• Visionary leader who clearly defines the desired outcome of the project and assembles the best team to execute the vision • Chief collaborator who facilitates the team's rapid formation to accelerate the team's productivity • Creates a culture of transparency and open information flow to ensure that all team members are working at optimum capacity • Addresses performance issues related to project • Provides feedback to team members at end of project to help them learn from the project and continuously improve • Completes administrative duties related to team-based incentives and social recognition	• Acts as a mentor and coach to help employees make the best decisions for themselves • Integrates feedback from different sources to help employees get a full picture of their performance during the year to inform their development plan based on the employees' career objectives • Coaches and advises the employees to complete their own development plans • Advocates for employees in promotions process based on their broad knowledge of employees' performance and aspirations • Completes administrative duties related to pay and performance

Where the activities of a manager within a function and the senior leader of a function depart is that the leader is able to focus on strategic planning for the function, building the capabilities required for the future, as well as resource management. Once again, the functional leader could leverage the Inside Gig and encourage individuals to take specific opportunities to build new capabilities that are needed in the organization. The leader could also promote other types of learning activities (e.g., attending conferences, hosting speakers, recommending books or articles). Functional leaders who are focused on the capabilities needed for the organization are likely to lead efforts to recruit external talent when the internal talent does not exist or cannot be developed in a timely manner.

PERSPECTIVES FROM THE INSIDE GIG

The Employee

Today's employees are focused on making a positive impact at work. Thus, they often show high levels of frustration when, early in their career, they are essentially told to wait on the sidelines until they have earned their stripes and the experience they need to become a manager. In a project-based work environment, all team members are respected for the contributions they can make to the team, regardless of their role in the company. It is possible for an employee to be identified as a project leader if they have the most appropriate skills on the team to lead the project. So this becomes a much more egalitarian approach to work.

Whether they take on a leadership role on a team or not, employees will build their own personal agility by being exposed to different types of projects, different project leadership styles, ideas from colleagues in different parts of the organization, and new experiences in general. This will help them develop greater personal flexibility in learning to listen to new and different perspectives and to adapt to the situation at hand.

Most importantly, the move from a strict reliance on traditional functional structures to integrating networks of teams to achieve project outcomes will provide more opportunities for employees to learn in the flow of real work. An employee may seek to be on a team because they are interested in learning something new or in advancing their skills by applying them in a different context. Whatever the situation, exposure to different types of projects will facilitate the continuous learning and growth that most millennials seek today.

The Manager

In a manager's world, customers are always changing their requirements and project initiatives go from being priority number one to yesterday's news in a blink of an eye. The ability to create a rapid response team to jump on a new, urgent customer problem is a huge benefit to managers. Typically, these issues require cross-company collaboration, and they are difficult to solve because the organization is not set up to work in this manner. But when ad hoc teams can be quickly formed to solve an emerging issue, the organization has a vehicle by which it can dynamically bring together the needed talent and then disband that team once the problem is solved. By leveraging technology that can use machine learning to match the talent within the organization to the needs of the project, managers can speed up the process by which they are able to address new problems.

Of course, not all work is tied to meeting an urgent business or customer need. Most work is focused on either maintaining existing systems or building new products to meet the emerging needs of current and potential future customers. Some teams may work together for a long period of time. Other teams may be formed to build something new that, once created, gets transferred to another team to embed the new work into the organization's regular, ongoing processes.

When managers are able to access *all* of the talent in the organization to solve a new problem or provide an alternative perspective to improve an existing process, they can deliver on their leadership's expectations. Today, organizations often access new perspectives offered by contractors, freelancers or consultants. While this may still be the case in the future, there are huge cost savings to the manager and the organization if they can leverage the talent within the organization to address organizational challenges. Since budget is always a major concern for managers, the ability to "borrow" talent from elsewhere in the organization should be highly attractive.

What is not attractive is the idea of loaning out "your" employees to help another part of the organization with their business challenges. However, consider the alternative. If your employees are not getting opportunities to learn and grow, they will leave; loaning them out for short assignments elsewhere in the company is better than losing them altogether. It also helps the organization to be more attractive to external candidates when the need arises to hire from outside.

The Company

Traditional organizational structures tend to have centralized decision-making, requiring information to cascade down the organization or slowly make its way up the chains of command. This structure can lead to slow decision-making, as information cannot make its way through the various levels in a timely manner. By creating networks of teams and empowering those teams to make decisions locally, an organization can increase the speed with which information flows through the organization and consequently speed up its decision-making ability. Today, organizations that can react quickly to changing business dynamics gain a competitive advantage. By empowering teams to make decisions, the company improves the organization's overall responsiveness, which in turn improves customer satisfaction and loyalty.

Lest the leaders of the company be concerned that all of their decision-making authority will be relinquished to teams, fear not! Governance structures at the top of the organization will still establish rules regarding who should be involved in making which decisions and what the limits are of decision-making authority. Senior leadership will always retain decision rights on big bets for the company and major investments in resources. It is not a choice between hierarchy at the top or teams. Rather, governance at the top creates the formal structures within which the organization can make responsible decisions, and decision-making is pushed down to the lowest levels possible to increase the organization's responsiveness and increase autonomy within the company. Increased autonomy will also make the organization more attractive to employees.

KEY TAKEAWAYS

- The Fourth Industrial Revolution, characterized by the rise of new technologies, is disrupting companies in every industry. In order for a company to compete, it will need to rethink and fundamentally reimagine its approach to business.

- The need to become more agile as individuals and organizations is clear. Organizations need to shift from traditional hierarchical structures (which are static and siloed; decision authority flows from the top down and they are often slow to change) to nimbler team-based structures that can form, expand and contract in response to changing customer demands.

- Agile organizations create fast-paced decision-making cultures because they empower teams to make decisions, and encourage teams to learn while doing and embed that learning within the organization.

- The growing complexity of work today is better suited to work that is completed in interdisciplinary teams that can address the many interwoven challenges posed through competing demands of different functions or customers.

- Team membership should be based on who has the skills to add value to the project or who needs to be part of the dialogue to optimize the outcome; team leadership is based on expertise and not position.

• People become more agile if they have a variety of experiences in different areas rather than focusing all their time on routine tasks and working with the same people.

• Organizations operating with team-based structures need to rethink the role of the manager. This role should be split into two: project leader (who leads the work) and career coach (the employee coach and advocate).

REFLECTION POINTS

Would you describe your organization as an agile one? Why or why not?

How much autonomy do teams have to make decisions?

Is cross-boundary access to skill sets part of your organization's culture?

What high-demand skills are required by your organization?

Is the role of manager working well in your organization? Do employees get the feedback and coaching they need to be successful, or are managers too busy "doing their job"?

CHAPTER 8
Principle No. 6: Bust the Functional Silos

Alone we can do so little; together we can do so much.
—Helen Keller

IMAGINE THAT YOUR COMPANY has envisioned the future of work and has taken steps to use its collective strengths to drive speed, agility, learning and execution. Faster, better, cheaper is the mantra of our time, and any barrier that stands in the way is knocked down. Authentic collaboration and the free flow of information are helping to solve complex problems. A new model of leadership acts on behalf of the entire enterprise.

The Fourth Industrial Revolution calls for open systems rather than closed ones, so traditional top-down management and organizational silos could be a silent organizational killer. To move toward a new way of working in networks of teams and breaking down traditional jobs, new organizational capabilities are needed and barriers must be removed. You need to "bust the functional silos" that block progress toward the open systems approach.

FROM THE FARM TO THE BOARDROOM

In agriculture, tall vertical structures called silos are built to store large amounts of grain. One silo houses one type of grain and another silo houses a different type. They are intentionally separated. In the business world, *organizational silos*, which are invisible structures, have a similar effect. They keep the different parts of an organization separated. The idea of concentrating like expertise in a silo to maximize productivity has unintentionally minimized resources and prevented information from being shared across departments and teams.[1]

Silos on farms do exactly what they're designed to do—store and separate various crops. In the business world, silos evolve as a natural outgrowth of the need to create order through structure and design of departments and functions. The premise of this way of thinking is that activities and tasks should be clustered in a way that concentrates specific work in a shared space. However, silos in organizations create barriers to the seamless flow of information, to the deployment of talent, and to building cultures of innovation, speed and agility.

Organizational Silos Defined .

A silo in a business context is an intangible structure created by collective mindsets that are primarily inward-looking and result in various levels of isolation and minimal cross-functional collaboration. In such an environment, employees sometimes draw the mistaken conclusion that it's not part of their job to coordinate their activities or interact with others outside of their group. Over time, they can even develop a belief that the work they do is all that should matter to them; therefore, they should not have to be concerned with the success of other teams and departments.

ORGANIZATIONS WITHOUT BOUNDARIES

Twenty-five or 30 years ago, working across organizational boundaries was an atypical way of thinking. Pioneered by Jack Welch, then CEO of General Electric (GE), this new way of thinking incorporated the idea that, in the 21st century, organizations would have to work in different ways in order to meet the requirements of growing globalization and technological innovation. Welch believed companies would have to adopt shorter decision cycles, increase employee engagement and strengthen collaboration to be competitive. His vision of a "boundaryless organization" led to the legendary GE Work-Out.[2] These were structured and facilitated sessions that brought diverse groups and teams from all parts of GE together for a common purpose—to solve problems and make decisions in real time. The Work-Outs also increased the opportunities for success through the diversity of thinking and perspectives brought to bear on problems.[3] This turned out to be a direct assault on silo thinking and behavior.

A 2019 *Harvard Business Review* article describes research to identify how employees make distinctions between the relationships they pay the most attention to versus the relationships they believe actually create the most customer value. The relationships employees pay the most attention to can be called "vertical chain of command structures," where someone is the leader or boss and everyone in that department or function reports to them. In such a structure, tasks are allocated to employees who work in the same part of the company. Conversely, the relationships that employees believe create customer value are those that cross organizational boundaries, or as the authors note, are "horizontal relationships."[4] This study points out a clear disconnect between customer and co-worker relationship priorities and where employees actually concentrate their time. An obvious question arises from these findings: Why does this disconnect—or what has become known as a silo mentality—appear to be so widespread?

WHY DOES A SILO MENTALITY DEVELOP?

If it was easy to pinpoint the causes of a silo mentality, it would likewise be easy to fix the problem. That said, some distinct factors contribute to the evolution of this type of thinking. One is the need for organizations to create order and structure to manage diverse complex projects. Diversity and complexity necessitate that projects be broken down into manageable chunks. Thus, it seems to be a logical division of labor to create teams and departmental functions, where sets of goals theoretically roll up to the larger team or departmental goals. However, despite the good intentions behind this concept, some unintended consequences can surface when it is implemented.

One consequence is an isolated focus on only those goals assigned to an individual or team, without consideration for the connections or interdependencies with goals outside of that area of accountability. This can result in a form of tunnel vision, which inhibits thinking strategically. It leads to thinking with only an up-and-down focus, rather than an up-and-down *and* across-boundaries focus.

Silo mentality *refers to an individual or an organization taking the most myopic view of a situation, circumstance or idea, which may only be relevant to their team or area of the business. Having a silo mentality means that you are likely to shut out alternative perspectives in favor of your own.*

A silo mentality is a product of culture. The powerful influence of company culture in shaping behavior is well known. Indeed, the culture of a company is a major force in determining whether it is successful or not. In one Bain & Co. study, the researchers found that 91 percent of the 1,200 senior executives at global companies surveyed agreed that "culture is as important as strategy for business success."[5] Consider the cultures of companies such as Apple, Southwest Airlines and Procter & Gamble, and their sustained success over time. Contrast that with the recent histories of companies like British Petroleum, Wells Fargo, Uber and Pacific Gas & Electric (PG&E) and the troubles that have plagued them. Much of the explanation for both sets of outcomes can be traced to company cultures that encourage specific behaviors that can lead to positive, or destructive, results. From these and other examples, it's clear that culture is a powerful influence in shaping employees' behaviors and expectations.

Leadership also has a bearing on the silo mentality. Along with culture, leadership is at the heart of a business. It is the bridge that connects visions and strategies with results. As complex as organizations are, most of what happens in them is ultimately traceable to culture and leadership. A famous quote by visionary thought leader Peter Drucker captures the role of leadership very succinctly: "The only thing that happens naturally in organizations is chaos, confusion and underperformance. Everything else requires leadership."[6] This observation succinctly sums up the reality that leadership commitment, action and follow-through are essential for sustainable changes of any magnitude to be realized.

Drucker adroitly places responsibility for most everything that occurs in a company at the feet of leadership. Leaders establish a tone and a set of values for a business culture. They let it be known—either by the explicitly rewarding particular behaviors, or by failing to change or eliminate other behaviors—exactly the kind of cultures they expect. So, despite widespread acknowledgment of the problems associated with a silo mentality, it continues to be a pervasive challenge for most organizations due to a failure of senior leadership to deal with the problem.

Another astute observer and chronicler of management activities notes that one paradox of the modern age is that while technology is in many ways integrating our world, it simultaneously creates new forms of fragmentation. Ironically, with data analytics bursting onto the scene of most companies, together with accelerated innovations and product development, these combined forces have created a set of activities and outputs that are often only understood by experts who themselves happen to reside in functional silos, whether they be in finance, engineering, operations, HR and so on.[7]

Consequences of a Silo Mentality

Where a silo mentality is a cultural norm, companies develop behaviors that can weaken trust, limit communication and even foster an "us versus them" way of thinking. One study published by SalesForce revealed that 70 percent of customer experience professionals, as well as executives, view a silo mentality as the biggest obstacle to a high standard of customer service.[8] When employees think and act primarily within the boundaries of their teams or departments without considering interdependencies or potentially valuable outside perspectives, it can have damaging implications for the business.

A silo mentality inadvertently reinforces localized and disconnected decision-making. In such a culture, there is no apparent benefit to collaboration, because goals are established primarily at the departmental or business unit level. Other departments or business units may have different and even competing goals, which are reinforced through various rewards and recognition programs. Therefore, there is no incentive for cross-functional problem solving.

Some reports regarding causes of the financial crisis that began in 2008 speculate that despite the fact that many very intelligent people were working in the financial sector at the time, and while most knew there were problems with structured commodities and mortgage-backed securities, no one took responsibility to raise concerns until the crisis was full-blown. In this example, a silo mentality created cultures that focused only on narrow segments of the larger organization, preventing cross-functional communication.[9]

A silo mentality also reduces efficiencies in overall business operations. The more disconnected teams or departments are from the full breadth of resources a company possesses, the more time, energy and money it will require to complete projects, solve customer problems, remove product development roadblocks and perhaps even execute strategic plans. These kinds of barriers can contribute to the development of "blaming cultures," where collective accountabilities are not adequately enforced or even acknowledged. In a blaming culture, finger pointing becomes a common response to the question of why certain expectations have not been met. It's a manifestation of a "we're all in this alone" mindset.

A silo mentality can breed a lack of trust and reinforce suspicions about the motivations of those outside one's work group. In extreme cases, teams or business units may begin to control the flow of information back and forth in order to protect their sense of purpose. Communication can suffer, or worse, intentionally slow down. Imagine an organization where collaboration is espoused as a good thing, but where the structure and culture actually discourage it. This is silo mentality at its worst. As author Patrick Lencioni succinctly states, "Silos—and the turf wars they enable—devastate organizations. They waste resources, kill productivity, and jeopardize the achievement of goals."[10]

BUSTING FUNCTIONAL SILOS TO CREATE ALIGNMENT

There are numerous strategies and recommendations for breaking down silos or a company's silo mentality. An often-cited one is the need to *create a unified vision*. This requires a commitment from leadership across the company that a free flow of information is in the best interests of achieving that vision.[11] In creating and articulating a unified vision, managers and employees must see the interconnectedness of their work and how their work impacts other parts of the business, including decisions that might inadvertently be made in a vacuum. They must come to understand that they are not separate pieces of a structure with ill-defined interdependencies. To avoid unintended consequences, it's important before embarking on a solution to check in with others who may be impacted further down the line. Managers and employees must also recognize that they are part of a larger talent supply chain, one that connects talent to the work that is required.

A second important recommendation for a silo-busting strategy is to *work toward achieving a common goal*. A unified vision must incorporate a clear articulation of how individuals, teams and departments all contribute to a common goal, which is bigger than their individual or team goals.

There is a famous story about President John F. Kennedy visiting NASA in the 1960s. At one point, he stopped and introduced himself to one of the janitors and asked him what his job was. Without hesitation, and with great conviction, the janitor responded, "I'm helping to put a man on the moon."[12] That janitor was absolutely clear about his role and how it connected to NASA's ultimate goal to put a man on the moon. Indeed, he believed that by keeping floors and offices clean, free of obstacles and garbage, he would be helping others to do their jobs more effectively, thereby facilitating the goal of a man on the moon by the end of the decade. Imagine if such clarity, focus and conviction of purpose were typical of all employees in all organizations.

All of the recommendations for busting silos include some form of "connecting" to other parts of a company as a central theme. Different words or phrases are used to describe this element—such as "assign cross-functional teams"[13] or "organize cross-silo dialogues"[14]—but they inevitably require stronger and deeper connections to people and functions outside of one's own area of work. This human element is a key link in the chain of actions necessary to break through a silo mentality and break down the barriers it creates.

Other silo-busting strategies include more frequent communication, realignment of rewards and recognition programs, more widespread use of collaboration tools, and the creation of cross-functional and multicultural teams. These are all positive actions that, when consistently executed well over time, can help to transform a culture where silos are the unwritten structures of behavior into one that values collaboration through connection. Collectively, these strategies are part of the "secret sauce" of unleashing organizational capacity.

THE LEADERSHIP IMPERATIVE

If this all sounds like a lot of work, that's because it is. However, leaders have to learn that if they keep doing the same things, they shouldn't expect different results. Let's not forget the underlying reasons for attempting to bust silos in the first place.

Think accelerated innovation, shorter product cycle times, quality improvements, rapid customer response and problem solving—all measurable results from opening up closed systems. These are competitive advantages that are a direct result of leveraging what's already available. One paradox of silo cultures is that while it may appear to be wise to enhance a business unit's perceived value and contribution by holding on to knowledge and resources, the potential for increasing that value and contribution is actually greater when you let go. The value of connecting people with similar areas of expertise so they can build off of one another is even further enhanced when that expertise is shared across organizational boundaries, thereby increasing the overall understanding of how different parts of a process impact each other.

Changing mindsets from *what is* to *what may be* holds the potential for both employee and organizational transformations. For employees, busting functional silos holds the promise of greater levels of engagement, increased contributions, and more widespread opportunities to use untapped talent capabilities. For organizations, research on the impact of collaboration has shown improvements in three key areas:

1. Innovation—product development and new business creation
2. Sales—cross-selling and customer service solutions
3. Operations—cost savings and improved decision-making[15]

Obviously, it's reasonable to consider redesigning organizational structures as a response to breaking silos. The field of organization development taught us long ago that structure influences behavior.[16] However, in considering structural redesign as a solution, it's important to use a realistic lens regarding the record of success in using this strategy. Said another way, simply "rearranging the deck chairs" may not yield the intended results. It's not uncommon for organizations to restructure in times of crisis or in response to newly established goals or strategies. In many cases, this is an appropriate action. However, if there's one essential ingredient of busting functional silos, it must be a genuine desire to change a restrictive cultural norm and minimize the barriers that sustain silo behavior. It must be a cultural aspiration and a leadership commitment.

Another important consideration is participation by key stakeholders. An often-cited research project by the Harvard Business School that explored the impact of early participation on reported feelings of ownership concluded that when people are involved in the early stages of a process, they will be more invested in that process over time.[17] This conclusion has become known as the "IKEA effect," because it was conducted with the IKEA company. This process clearly demonstrated the power of inclusion and participation in facilitating real change. If you want employees to make changes in their behavior, solicit their input about the changes you are hoping to achieve. Get them involved in the planning and design of what's required to shift behaviors, then work to sustain the desired changes over time. Ask them what they think. Ask them if they believe the changes are necessary and how they will benefit them and the company. Then ask for their commitment and watch the progress.

 The IKEA effect *refers to a research project done with IKEA that looked at the impact of early participation in a project and the positive impact early participation had on stakeholders and their feeling of ownership of the project.*

The glue that binds this kind of effort together must be to explain and obtain agreement on the "why" behind the change. When people understand why they're being asked to change their behavior, even if they disagree with the change, they're more likely to make the shift.[18] Asking why reveals the underlying intentions behind what we do or ask others to do. It lets people know the rationale, so they don't draw the wrong conclusions. In the absence of complete information, people have a tendency to make up what they don't know or don't understand, thereby completing the story behind the request for themselves. Describing why can minimize how much the story is filled in with incorrect information.

REVISITING THE ROLE OF COLLABORATION

By now, it should be clear that the existence of silos in business served a purpose at one point in time—to organize and bring together people with common areas of expertise. However, in today's complex organizations, solutions to problems are rarely one-dimensional. Thus, the need for cross-silo collaboration has grown increasingly important. Working from that premise, and considering the various approaches and strategies for breaking down silo behavior, we would be remiss not to dive deeper regarding the role of collaboration in the attempt to shift silo behaviors.

Collaboration is at the heart of cross-functional behavior. It's the vehicle upon which opening up channels of communication depends if tangible benefits to working outside of one's team or business unit are to be achieved. Here's what we believe about collaboration in today's business world:

- The more decentralized companies become, the greater the need for collaboration.
- The more companies use cross-functional teams or matrix structures, the greater the need for collaboration.
- The more global or complex companies become, the greater the need for collaboration.
- The more companies work to break down silo behaviors, the greater the opportunity for collaboration.

This growing need for greater levels of collaboration has also spawned an abundance of collaboration tools that are now on the market. Here are just a few of them: Confluence, Connecteam, Dropbox, GoToMeeting, Google Hangouts, Google Team Drive, Huddle, Slack, Skype, Workplace, Webex, Yammer, and Zoom.

This ever-growing list of collaboration solutions is a market-fueled response to the issues that come up in attempting to bust functional silos. They constitute part of the "how" of opening up communication channels, of increasing participation across boundaries, and of stimulating innovation and creative problem solving. However, it is our belief that collaboration without purpose is *not* a desired solution. In other words, collaboration for its own sake—so the company can point to widespread involvement of others and claim, "See, we encourage collaboration here"—should not be the goal of real collaborative efforts.

141

> For collaboration to be effective, it must have a purpose, a reason
> for encouraging it beyond simply getting people involved. Don't mis-
> understand the point here. Involvement is ordinarily a good thing, but
> unnecessary involvement by too many people can lead to decision-
> making paralysis and a drawn-out process of never-ending discus-
> sions. The key to effective collaboration is knowing how and when to
> use it. Effective collaboration is also knowing when *not* to use it.

As Morten Hansen writes in his book *Collaboration*, there are key questions to decide on a collaboration effort, for example, to clarify its benefits. One such question is: What's the upside for the company and for employees if we collaborate on this particular project? Other variables that will help determine if collaboration is the right action include identifying the potential barriers in the company that may inhibit or prevent effective collaborative efforts. Such factors as the current mindsets of those involved, as well as existing trust levels between departments or business units, are important considerations here.

Being clear regarding what people need to be effective when collaborating with others is also a key component. These questions deal with the best ways to match people and work. The consideration here should *not* be to encourage more collaboration, but rather to ensure that the right people are matched to the right tasks. So, while collaboration may be desirable, it is not always be the right action or the best way to achieve a goal.

THE OPEN SYSTEM IS THE FUTURE

In today's hyper-paced business environments, with increased levels of uncertainty and an ever-growing need to tap the untapped value contributions of the workforce, functional silos do not support the shifts that characterize the future of work. Silos represent an older mindset that discourages the free flow of information and resources. They set up artificial barriers to leveraging the vast pool of internal talent in every company. They slow down, restrict and sometimes block innovation and the agility goals that most companies now embrace.

The Fourth Industrial Revolution requires more open systems, not closed ones. It requires more frequent and faster communication, not roadblocks of structure or mindset. Companies that thrive in this emerging revolution will have permeable boundaries, loosely coupled networks of expertise, employees who move in and out of assignments, and an open exchange of ideas and talent. This will require a new way of thinking, a new vision of work and new ideas about organizational structures that perhaps don't yet exist. To "bust the functional silos" is one important stepping stone to creating that future of work, and it needs to start now!

PERSPECTIVES FROM THE INSIDE GIG

The Employee

Functional silos present barriers for employees in many ways. They can breed feelings of isolation and mistrust of others outside of one's own team or department. They prevent open and free-flowing communication between teams, departments and business units. They minimize collaboration, which in turn impedes innovation and collective problem solving. They create and reinforce mindsets that can be in stark contrast to the espoused values of a company, particularly those that promote collaboration and agility. In short, there is no justifiable benefit for employees who work in cultures where a silo mentality and its related behaviors exist. Busting functional silos opens up possibilities. It reinforces open cultures with cross-functional lines of communication, promoting a "we're all in this together" mindset. It helps to facilitate work by creating access to the wide range of resources versus talent being "owned" by one functional leader.

The Manager

With workloads and complexity increasing, managers often find them-selves struggling to keep up. They have significant responsibilities to complete project work, to manage teams of employees and to deliver on their portion of strategic accountabilities. They must do this while frequently not having access to everything that's needed to fulfill those responsibilities. Ironically, what managers need may often exist across the hall, across the street or perhaps in another geographic location. They and their bosses must also try to align and coordinate large amounts of work that support the company vision and strategic plan. That can be extremely challenging without open communication chan-nels and sharing of relevant information, resources and talent. Func-tional silos prevent managers from accessing much of what is needed to deliver on their accountabilities. This can compound time pressures, and in some cases affect the quality and thoroughness of work. Con-versely, working across silos can create greater efficiencies as employees across departments understand the impacts of each other's work. The outcome is that the best solution or product can be developed the first time.

The Company

Work as we know it is fundamentally changing. The structures and processes that have shaped how companies operate are being disrupted. The work is more complex than ever before, necessitating the collabo-ration of people not only across organizational functions, but also across organizational boundaries. Faster, better, cheaper is the mantra of our time, and any type of barrier to those marching orders must be evaluated to determine its impact. If it's determined that such bar-riers stand in the way of innovation, agility and competitiveness, then they should be minimized or eliminated altogether. This requires a compelling vision for the company, a set of well-articulated and col-lectively understood goals, a talent supply chain that matches the skill requirements needed, and a set of values and behaviors that reinforces a new mindset about work. It also requires raising the bar for leadership, because good enough isn't good enough anymore!

KEY TAKEAWAYS

- Organizational structures have always been tied to the goals of creating order, increasing operational efficiencies, stimulating performance improvements, removing barriers to work, eliminating redundancies and generally supporting what is in the best interests of a business. Sometimes, structural changes are beneficial and yield positive benefits. Sometimes they do not. Businesses should regularly evaluate the ROI of existing structures to determine if a change may be necessary.

- Functional silos have developed for a variety of reasons. Ultimately, they represent a failure to act for the benefit of the enterprise, but instead to act for the benefit of a team, a department or a business unit. This is not only a cultural issue, but also a failure of leadership to address a problem.

- Solutions to busting functional silos include creating unifying visions, working toward common goals, realigning rewards and encouraging the use of more cross-functional teams along with more frequent communications.

- More effective collaboration across organizational boundaries holds the promise of improved communication, elimination of redundancies, stronger levels of trust between functions, greater levels of innovation, increased business acumen due to an understanding of impacts on other parts of the business, and a variety of other benefits. Surely these are desirable results. By paying particular attention to the ways in which collaboration can be maximized, companies create opportunities for measurable improvements in organizational health and in building high-performance cultures.

REFLECTION POINTS

How would you assess the flow of information in your company? Are there barriers to getting access to information?

Have you taken or are you able to take leadership initiatives to diminish the effects of a silo mentality?

If you are in a progressive company that has worked to encourage authentic collaboration, what outcomes have you seen?

Looking into the future, what steps might your organization take to create greater collaboration across organizational boundaries?

PART THREE
How to Make It Work

Creative thinking inspires ideas. Ideas inspire change.
—Barbara Januszkiewicz

CHAPTER 9
A New Talent Operating Model: Rethinking Ways of Working

Leaders in an execution culture design strategies
that are more road maps than rigid paths.
—Ram Charan

THE SIX PRINCIPLES THAT UNDERPIN the Inside Gig act to create a shift in mindset of an organization from one of scarcity to one of abundance (Principle No. 1: "You get what you give"); introduce the notion of skills inventories to better manage talent (Principle No. 2: "Know what you have"); create a culture of continuous learning and expanded job experience (Principle No. 3: "Create a learning organization"); give employees increased choice (Principle No. 4: "Democratize the work"); design organizations for speed and responsiveness (Principle No. 5: "Create an agile organization"); and break down silos that inhibit opportunity and innovation (Principle No. 6: "Bust the functional silos"). All of these principles speak to higher cross-collaboration and the intelligent use of talent, including talent that the organization discovers among its people.

As shown in Figure 1.1 Operating Model (see page 18, chapter 1), one component of the talent operating model is the *ways of working* that support the move to an Inside Gig, project-based work environment, which enables the more fluid use of talent across the organizations. This chapter will focus on those ways of working, and the next one will address the *people and process* capabilities of the talent operating model. Throughout this chapter and the next, we will use *talent platform* as the generic term for a technology solution that facilitates this new way of working.

Think of chapters 9 and 10 as a user's guide to how to operate under these new conditions. We recognize that people will implement the Inside Gig approach to talent mobility at different stages of maturity in implementing project-based work. The anticipated stages of workplace transformation are described in Table 9.1 Maturity Phases of the Inside Gig Talent Operating Model. At the outset, the table shows how a company may begin if is new to project-based work. The second stage is appropriate for companies that are gaining comfort not only with project-based work but also with creating gigs inside of the company. We anticipate that it could take an organization 5 to 15 years to transition to the highest level of maturity with the Inside Gig model. In this future state, companies will be sharing talent across internal boundaries and also within their business partner ecosystem.

Table 9.1 Maturity Phases of the Inside Gig Talent Operating Model

Relatively New to Project-Based Work	Gaining Comfort with the Inside Gig	Workplace 2030+
Begin implementing a talent platform solely for development purposes or simultaneously in parts of the organization that are quite used to working in a project-based work structure. If this is a large organization, roll out the talent platform in parts of the company that display the most readiness, and create pull by other parts of the company as successes are shared across the organization.	**Managers are more comfortable with project-based work** and more functions begin to operate this way. **The organization integrates its internal and external processes for selecting for project-based work** (with a preference for internal employees). This allows internal employees to work part-time, providing new work options for women and older employees.	Companies leverage the talent platform to **share talent with strategic business partners,** taking business collaborations a step further and accelerating innovation by bringing together different areas of expertise to solve common problems. This takes the concept of the boundaryless organization to a whole new level.

Learning to seamlessly leverage both external talent (contractors) and internal talent takes a fair bit of thought from a manager. A manager needs to consider not only what work makes sense to be done to move a project forward, but within that work how the company's core skill set can be applied and how external contractors' competencies can be used. External contractors can deliver highly specialized skills for a short period, as required by the company, and they can also complement capacity on non-core capabilities on an as-needed basis that allows employees to focus on what they do best.

Many companies today operate in a business environment that is so competitive that it requires significant amounts of collaboration within the company to win in the marketplace. We can imagine a future that takes this further. In the future, organizations may come together to form *heterarchies*, which Karen Stephenson defines as "collaborative endeavors of organizations that are networked together. While each organization may have its own internal hierarchy, neither one has control over the other, but they work together for shared goals."[1] This goes beyond the idea of a consortium (joint ownership that does not include sharing of any information or talent across organizational boundaries). In a heterarchy, the relationship across the companies is highly collaborative, and the focus is on the delivery of a common goal. This is collaboration in its highest form.

This vision may sound inconceivable—even competitors may be bedfellows. But examples of this type of talent sharing across organizational boundaries between strategic partners have been cited in business literature, notably in the book *Lead the Work: Navigating a World Beyond Employment* by John Boudreau, Ravin Jesuthasan and David Creelman.[2] One example they share is a strategic partnership between Disney and Siemens. When Siemens was challenged to figure out how to market hearing aids to children (not their usual target market), they turned to their strategic partner, the world's best marketer to children. Disney marketing employees assigned to the Siemens project came up with the concept of marketing the hearing aid like a toy—with a stuffed animal and a storybook—and not like a medical device. This project was a win-win. The product was a marketplace success for Siemens, and Disney got a share in the profits because the marketing relied on its intellectual property (Disney characters).

Through this partnership, Siemens could tap into the best available talent to innovate a marketing solution.

GONE ARE THE OLD WAYS OF WORKING: SHIFTING THE CULTURE

Traditional organizations are built on hierarchies that have a deep history. Employees climb the corporate ladder with the requisite trappings of their growing status. With or without the talent platform, these traditional structures are starting to crumble under a new set of employee values that respect *accomplishment* over *authority*, because authority may or may not be merited. Companies are getting flatter and job titles matter less as everyone focuses on the work that lies ahead. Most people would argue that we will always have some form of hierarchy to help organize resources. While that may be true, it would be wise for employees to refrain from coveting their job titles too much. The freelance marketplace would indicate that skills, experiences and reputation will be the job currency of the future.

As we saw in discussing Principle No. 1, "You get what you give," organizations need to embrace a mindset shift from "my employees" to "the company's talent." This *abundance mindset* helps managers look beyond their direct reports to solve problems and allows their employees to explore their passions and interests across other groups, teams or departments within the organization. This sense of being *boundary-less* as an organization enhances a company's ability to innovate, because people from a diversity of disciplines are brought together to tackle problems from numerous perspectives. Team leaders can bring in new skill sets that add value and enhance work products to make them more valuable to the consumer. A culture that considers all talent a company asset, and that allows and expects people to move seamlessly across the organization from project to project, brings with it a group of employees who are well rounded, understand the company as a whole, and have a broader perspective than just their single function.

The Shift to New Leadership Behaviors

To enable people to pursue their passions for new challenges and stretch opportunities through a new talent operating model, six leadership behaviors are necessary. They will help overcome the cultural norms that resist the change in behavior required to successfully implement this type of organizational change. These behaviors are of equal importance; they are listed in no particular order. However, more important than any single behavior listed here is that leadership must be 100 percent behind this type of strategic initiative. It is a significant shift in how talent is utilized in the organization. Senior leaders especially must role-model these behaviors to everyone in the company.

- **Develop others:** Leaders must facilitate the development of their people, even if this means giving them some time away from their core job responsibilities. While we understand that at times it is "all hands on deck" to cross the finish line on a project, every day should not be like this. It should be realistic to give employees many opportunities for personal development.

- **Foster collaboration:** Working with the same group of people day in, day out can lead to deep friendships and strong, resilient teams. But new perspectives to solve challenging problems can spark breakthrough solutions. Leaders who encourage people to work together with others from across the organization will help drive greater innovation, which is needed to win in the marketplace. One benefit of this new talent operating model is to find the hidden talent in the organization that can contribute in new ways to help the company (and the employees) be more successful. Great leaders foster a collaborative culture among their employees.

- **Be inclusive:** Inclusiveness is associated with collaboration, because collaboration requires people to be more inclusive of others who are different and who might think or work differently. This involves reaching across organizational silos to find talent in non-intuitive places that can be leveraged in new and different ways. The more relationships individuals can build across the organization, the greater the likelihood that they can access the knowledge or resources needed for a project to be successful. "Be inclusive" is also about providing a way for employees to contribute on their own terms, which may enable an organization to access a broader pool of talent. This is especially valuable as the talent supply gets tighter.

- **Let go (be flexible):** Give employees more freedom and flexibility to *choose* the projects they want to work on. Don't hold employees back because you feel pressure to get "your" work done. When managers allow their employees to work on another project or opportunity, they should turn to the talent platform to get the additional talent needed to work on their projects and make up for their reduction in resources. In addition, not every moment is a busy one. Take advantage of slack times and encourage employees to find projects that tap into their passions, interests or areas they want to develop. Employees will respond to being able to contribute to compelling side projects by working hard and committing to the organization.

- **Be transparent:** In a digital world, it is hard to keep information from getting out to a broader audience than you intend. While this may be a fact of life today, it is more about how you use information at work and your underlying motives. Information is to be shared, not used for power. Those who try to hoard information to gain power will lose their employees' trust and confidence. Because work is distributed in teams, the teams need to have access to information and they need to understand *why* decisions were made above them, so that they can integrate this understanding into how they approach their work. There must be a free flow of information to ensure that everyone is aligned. Transparency does not mean sharing intellectual property with people who do not have the proper agreements with the company, and it does not mean sharing sensitive data. It is about being open about what decisions need to be made, by whom and how they will be made, and when employees will be notified so that they can do their work fully informed of the context.

- **Think strategically:** The Inside Gig talent operating model, introduced in chapter 1, is different from the model of companies that permit employees to work on projects of their own choosing strictly to foster innovation within the company. The Inside Gig connects skills of current employees to current projects that are focused on executing the organization's business strategy. Thus, it is important not to be myopic about one's own project. Each project should be strategically relevant to moving the business forward. Where possible, work should connect to other relevant projects to share learnings.

The Shift to Agile Decision-Making

As the organization shifts from a strictly functionally driven leadership to a structure that is more focused on project-based work, more empowerment and freedom must be given to the team. Everyone on the project team must own the project outcome, so they all must act as leaders. They need to know exactly why decisions are being made above them because it may impact how they go about their work. This serves to make the transparency aspect of leadership behaviors more obvious when it comes to decision-making.

For example, if a team has been given a project, then the team needs to be able to make decisions up to a predetermined scope or dollar amount. The team cannot constantly have its decisions checked with multiple leaders from different parts of the business. Matrixed work structures requiring approval from all leaders will kill this type of process. Decision-making needs to be as agile as the teams. Decisions need to be made quickly, within clear parameters. The organization needs to establish a clear process that will match the rhythm of the project.

It is imperative to establish early on the agreed-upon process for issue resolution. Usually authority is given to the most appropriate individual who has the information to make the best determination. In a highly collaborative organization, a common process is one in which everyone is provided with the opportunity to provide input, and then after careful consideration of all points of view, the team leader becomes the final arbitrator.

The Shift in Organization Design

As discussed in chapter 7, Principle No. 5: Create an Agile Organization, companies need to shift from a strict reliance on hierarchy and move to more team-based work structures that can grow, shrink and change based on emerging needs. But Rome was not built in a day, nor is the way organizations are structured going to fundamentally change with one click of the keyboard. It will take time to become agile.

Traditional organizational hierarchies do still serve an important role in organizations. They bring governance to how employees are organized within the company, how profit-and-loss accountabilities are aligned and distributed, and who needs to be involved in significant strategic conversations. The senior management team (depending on the size of your organization, this could involve several layers of management—C-suite leaders, general managers, executive vice presidents, senior vice presidents, and vice presidents) still need to guide the organization's strategy and determine how different parts of the organization will come together to execute the business strategy.

Thus, it is not a choice of either a hierarchical structure or networks of teams working together to move the organization forward—it is both. These two structures can live side-by-side. The hierarchical structure serves as the governing body of the organization. It makes decisions that cut across the organizations, determines resourcing and budgets within a function, and identifies when new capabilities need to be brought into the organization to execute strategic goals. Teams are formed to address important projects or emerging customer issues that require collaboration. These teams are not permanent structures; they form and dissolve on an as-needed basis. Project teams enable employees to join a project that is outside of their regular job, thus bringing employees variety and choice. Sure, some employees will be assigned to work on specific projects because of the knowledge or skills they must contribute to the project, but projects also provide an opportunity for choice.

MOVING FROM JOBS TO PROJECT-BASED WORK

The most challenging aspect of the move from job-based work systems to project- or task-based work systems is not the technology that facilitates the process or the data structures that the entire system sits upon. It is the act of taking what has been a full-time job and figuring out how to break it down into a series of projects or tasks that can be distributed to a different set of people.

There are multiple ways to approach breaking down a job into discrete projects. First, think about any given job description. Are there elements of a job description that are unique, where skills could be distilled into distinct parts that could be performed by a qualified person? If so, then those unique aspects could be applied to individual projects. And a project can often be further broken down into discrete tasks that make up the project. These tasks can be turned into opportunities for an employee to contribute to a project in more bite-size chunks. This is largely the way that on-demand talent platforms operate today. You can hire a videographer to film a presentation and then hire a separate editor to cut that video and add sound to create flashy marketing collateral.

Here's another way of thinking about it. Think about a job as a pie. Are there slices that can be given to someone else, so that an individual can focus on those slices of the pie, or the job, that they are best suited to execute? Also, most people do not love all aspects of their current role. But the tasks one person may not like (e.g., developing a PowerPoint presentation) may be another person's passion (perhaps it enables them to tap into their creative talents). Project planning may drive some project leaders crazy, but other employees may love planning and organizing and thrive on doing this type of work. Moving the work around to those people who thrive in doing that type of work lets everyone do their best work at their highest level of engagement.

157

Example: The Project Manager Position

Most people are familiar with the role of a project manager. While there may be many ways to break an activity into projects, these are two common approaches.

Approach 1: Play Favorites with Your Projects

A project manager may manage anywhere from one to seven different projects during the year. Some of these projects will be large and consume a significant percentage of their time, while others will be smaller and simpler (making them great learning experiences for people wanting to gain experience in a skill set). Some of these projects will be in areas the project manager is deeply passionate about, while others will be something they do because they can, not because they are driven to engage on the project.

Smaller learning-size projects and projects that don't particularly engage a project manager are high-quality options to offer to others. They might be a perfect fit for others to learn or express their passion.

Approach 2: Discover Your Strengths,
Play to Them, and Create Opportunities for Others

Project managers often have a variety of different job responsibilities, some of which are their strong suit and some of which are not. Executing the Inside Gig concept is an opportunity to deconstruct a traditional job into its key elements and then redistribute the work to the most qualified, or most deeply engaged, employees for that work. Let's look at the key elements of the project manager role.

- Plan the project: Define the scope, work plan, resources and schedules, etc.
- Staff the project: Recruit, interview and select staff; manage project staff.
- Implement the project: Monitor project execution and establish communication schedules and processes.

- Control the project: Develop and manage project budget; prepare financial reports.
- Evaluate the project: Review if project was on time, on budget and met quality levels; document key learnings.

A project manager may, for example, be great at all aspects of this work except for the financial planning and budgeting aspects of the work. If the job is deconstructed, this work could be an opportunity for another individual whose expertise and passion is financial analysis. Alternatively, perhaps the project manager is great with numbers, but not as great with the people aspects. Having someone to partner with on the staffing aspects of the role would help the project manager enjoy the job much more and expose another employee to aspects of project management.

To sum up, a new talent operating model is needed to fully leverage the Inside Gig concept. While it is possible to simply implement technology to offer gigs to current employees, it is only when a company fully embraces the Inside Gig model by aligning all of the ways the company operates to support this new way of working that the company can realize the full value of this talent operating model.

KEY TAKEAWAYS

- To adopt this new talent operating model, organizations must adapt their ways of working to support a more fluid approach to talent mobility.

- A culture that is modeled by leaders speaks volumes to the way work gets accomplished in an organization. A culture that supports the Inside Gig would contain the following elements:

› Accomplishment over authority: While today's employees may covet their job titles, the freelance marketplace suggests that skills, experiences and reputation will be the job currency of the future.

› Abundance mindset: Managers view the company's collective talent as a whole and look across the business to meet short-term needs.

› Boundarylessness: Individuals are encouraged to contribute where they can add value regardless of their department or role.

› Continuous learning culture: Both managers and employees value and support ongoing learning opportunities.

› Follow your passion: Employees can choose to contribute to work they are passionate about.

• To communicate expectations for the new ways of working, leadership behaviors are adopted that set new expectations: develop others, foster collaboration, be inclusive, let go (be flexible), be transparent, and think strategically.

• Decision-making processes must push the authority for decisions down to the team level to ensure teams have the autonomy and authority to move quickly.

• Organizational structures must be realigned to ensure that stability does not come at the expense of agility.

• Most importantly, companies must develop the skills to break jobs down into projects/tasks.

REFLECTION POINTS

Do you see pressure building to change the way projects are managed in your workplace?

It is one thing to think about how your own people collaborate, but have you thought of collaborating in some way with other companies that are your strategic partners?

Is the culture in your workplace conducive to employees contributing on their own terms? Is it perhaps partway there, or can it never happen? Why?

Are teams created for specific and evolving business demands, or are teams static in their makeup? What do you think are the pros and cons?

CHAPTER 10
A New Talent Operating Model: Capability Alignment

The reason why it is so difficult for existing firms to capitalize on disruptive
innovations is that their processes and their business model that make them good at
the existing business actually make them bad at competing for the disruption.
—Clayton Christensen

THIS CHAPTER ADDRESSES the *people and process* capabilities needed
to support the Inside Gig talent operating model and the implementation of a talent platform technology. The People Capabilities
section largely focuses on the staffing model needed to implement this
new approach to work and the communications required to facilitate
this way of working. In the Process Capabilities section, we suggest
how current HR processes need to be aligned to reinforce and support
talent mobility and the movement toward more project-based work
structures.

PEOPLE CAPABILITIES

While there are many subjects we could address under the People
category, we have chosen to focus on two categories: Project Management and Communications. The former is largely about the resource
requirements to implement the Inside Gig talent operating model. The
latter is to ensure that some critical communications processes are
established that will help this effort be successful.

Project Management

To implement a talent platform that facilitates talent mobility and to manage the process, a dedicated project manager is highly recommended. This is a process, not unlike performance management or compensation, that will need ongoing attention to ensure it optimizes the allocation of talent in the organization. Attracting people to the system and getting managers comfortable with giving employees freedom to choose their own projects will be a journey for any organization. It will help mitigate the challenges to have a dedicated full-time individual who manages the process. It is also necessary to have someone who oversees information and data that are entered into the system to ensure that they meets the intended goals and expectations for the types of projects you expect on the platform, and to measure the outcomes of the process so that the organization can assess its impact.

Selecting Employees through the Talent Platform

Experience tells us that if you make the employee selection process as onerous as the company's hiring process, it will fail. Employees who wish to engage in projects should not be put off by an unduly rigid process. It needs to be as easy as a click of a button to apply for a project. Most of the employee's information should already be attached to their profile. For a manager, selecting an employee should be as easy as selecting a movie on Netflix.

Just because the process is simple to use, with no apparent checks and balances, does not mean that it is a system unchecked. HR does need to ensure fairness and make sure all employees get equal access to opportunities. Advanced analytic capabilities enabled through this process will ensure that data can be regularly monitored and course corrections can be made if any bias or favoritism is found in the system.

Communications

Employee-Manager Communications

When employees look for opportunities on the platform, they will likely think about how they are to communicate with others regarding potential projects. One frequent question we hear when companies consider implementing this type of talent operating model in their organization is: When should an employee let their manager know that they are looking at an opportunity? When they are thinking about it? Before they apply? If they are asked for an interview? Only if they accept an offer?

While every company needs to establish its own procedures related to notification, based on our experience, we offer the following advice. Employees should not be required to notify their manager if they are exploring possible projects or opportunities on the talent platform. This applies whether they are just thinking about it or even applying for a potential project opportunity. Lots of people go on informational interviews. Once an employee has been vetted for the opportunity and there is mutual agreement (from both the project manager and the employee) that they are a good fit, only then should an employee have a conversation with their current manager about making room for the new project.

Team-Based Management

As the organization progresses more toward working in teams, it is critical to have an open flow of communication not only within the teams that will be forming and disbanding on a regular basis, but also between teams that touch related processes. There are probably hundreds of tools available to help an organization facilitate the communication across networks of teams (see chapter 8 for examples).

If an organization does not decide on a common collaboration platform quickly, be assured that employees will adopt their own. These platforms are readily available and inexpensive for small teams.

PROCESS CAPABILITIES

While most of what we will discuss here pertains to what will happen both today and in the next five years, the long-term vision for a talent platform is that it helps the chief human resources officer become the chief operating officer of the talent supply chain. However, this requires an organization to consider the complete human cloud of talent, which is both internal and external to the organization, extending beyond organizational boundaries to partner organizations as well as leveraging other talent platforms for highly specialized talent.

Many HR processes are impacted by the implementation of this type of technology. This operating model will address each process and make recommendations for how to take advantage of the shifts the organization will need to make in the way it works to better attract, engage, develop and retain top talent.

Resource Deployment

This talent operating model will help managers find talent internally so that they can quickly execute. Contrast this with the amount of time it would take to complete a requisition to hire a contractor on the external market and to go through the procurement process. For very short-term projects, an organization can deploy its own internal resources much more quickly than it can even access the talent externally. Even for longer-term projects, it makes more sense to leverage the talent a company already has than to go external and pay more for additional resources.

As we discussed in chapter 7, Principle No. 5: Create an Agile Organization, in the future, teams will quickly form and disband to address business challenges and needs. A core group of internal employees will move from team to team to share their skills to achieve their teams' goals. In addition to this core team of internal employees, in the future we anticipate the organization more fluidly bringing in external resources on a just-in-time basis to meet specific business needs. Some of these skills will be core to the business, but difficult (if not impossible) for a company to secure as full-time employees because these individuals do not want to work for one employer. Other employees will not be core to the business, and the organization will utilize them to optimize work so that employees are able to focus on what they do best. Other tasks will be outsourced to more effectively utilize business resources.

Each organization will need to create its own "rules of the road" for deploying resources. While many organizations are leveraging the Inside Gig concept for development purposes only, and assuming that employees have some slack time available to contribute to other projects while achieving their core job responsibilities, in chapter 3, Principle No. 1: You Get What You Give, we addressed the idea of explicit talent sharing. Companies adopting this approach have operated under the understanding that if an employee works on a project under a different cost center for 1 percent to 20 percent of their time, budgets can accommodate these reallocations in resources (meaning, there are no changes to budgets under these circumstances). Once an employee is spending more than 30 percent of their time in another part of the organization, managers who are responsible for their own budgets grow uncomfortable with the loss of resources. At this point, managers may need to work out some type of resource sharing if a project is going to last for a long period of time. However, recall that "you get what you give." If a manager is losing resources to another team, they can post projects in the talent platform to acquire the resources to fill those gaps or others.

Team Development

While in the talent platform, employees are likely to come together as a small group of individuals with complementary skills who are committed to a common goal and who are all held mutually accountable to the outcomes of the project. Special attention should be paid to accelerating the formation of these teams so that they can become productive as quickly as possible.

A clear, specific goal will provide the team with a common sense of purpose. That sense of purpose, in turn, is essential to forming a cohesive team. Successful teams spend as much time investing in developing an agreed-upon approach for *how* they will work together as they do in clearly defining their purpose. This must include both the administrative aspects of how they will communicate and ultimately document their work, as well as how they will divide up responsibilities for various tasks.

The norms, or collective behaviors, that teams share must be quickly established. Recent research has pointed us to two not very surprising norms (or behaviors) that govern highly effective teams. The first norm is around spending equal amounts of time talking in the group, or *conversational turn-taking*. This means there is not one overbearing individual in the group who is dominating the conversation, or two people who volley back and forth like a good tennis match, without allowing anyone else to enter the conversation. The group must agree at the beginning that all members will be allowed to voice their opinions, and they will do so by taking turns so that they are equally contributing to the discussion.

The second norm is around having *social sensitivity*, being able to intuit how others are feeling based on their body language, tone of voice or other nonverbal expressions. Some people are adept at picking up on social cues and nonverbal behaviors, while other cohorts have a reputation for being less sensitive. So it may take additional effort for some people to become in tune with their peers' nonverbal behaviors. Peer feedback and coaching can help these individuals gain greater sensitivity to others.

Amy Edmondson from Harvard Business School has published research on psychological safety, which is often composed of elements including conversational turn-taking and social sensitivity.[1] She defines *psychological safety* as "a shared belief held by members of a team that the team is safe for interpersonal risk-taking and the team will not embarrass, reject or punish someone for speaking up." Creating such a group culture of respect is what helps a team get comfortable quickly and move toward action in a manner that is fulfilling to all involved.

While some teams may form for a day or a week, others may be together for a year or more. We recommend creating a team quick-start kit to facilitate the teams getting themselves to productivity quickly. The kit should address issues such as team vision, goal clarity, clarifying roles and responsibilities, establishing team norms and decision-making processes.

Performance Management

Performance management needs a complete refresh under any circumstances, let alone in the context of the changes associated with the new ways of working. In a future world where employees move from project to project, there is no way for an employee's manager to have insight into their overall performance to provide an annual review. So, the approach to this very traditional, outdated process must be rethought.

Even for employees who are still primarily working in a traditional hierarchical structure and in one well-defined role, the growing complexity of work requires more and more collaboration across the business. Thus, we believe that getting crowdsourced feedback or feedback from colleagues will be more important. Also, by leveraging new technologies and AI capabilities, companies will be able to gather real-time performance data, enabling ongoing conversations about performance.

We suggest that to support this new talent operating model, organizations consider the following attributes as part of how they manage performance going forward.

- Everyone should have clear, specific, measurable goals.

  › When possible, individual goals should be shared with team members; when everyone knows what others are focused on and where common accountabilities intersect, they can collaborate.

- Each project team should have goals that team members collectively agree to achieve.

  › Team metrics should be used where appropriate and shared for everyone to see. This way accountability for success is transparent.

169

- The process should incorporate feedback from each project manager the employee works with during the year. (Real-time performance metrics are gathered when available.)

- The process should consider real-time crowdsourced feedback from project teammates. It is also possible to incorporate feedback from external partners. At a minimum, feedback should be gathered at the end of each project. Feedback may focus on skills demonstrated, collaboration or living the company values.

- Throughout the year, a career coach should help the employee synthesize the feedback they've received and help to identify key trends/issues to help guide individual development.

- Use technology to automate the integration of data sources, to build an ongoing summary of performance.

- Create greater automated connections, via AI technologies, of performance management outcomes into learning offerings.

- More and more performance management processes have changed from a focus on evaluation to a focus on coaching and development, emphasizing a *growth mindset* where all employees can achieve a great deal with the right type of support and information. Rather than reviewing goals to evaluate performance, upcoming goals are reviewed to help coach and support employees to fuel their success.

Feedback from managers and teammates can begin to serve as the foundation of a person's digital reputation within the company. Project leaders will evaluate employees along specific dimensions such as teamwork and technical, problem solving and communication skills. Employees may also have the opportunity to rate project leaders for their project leadership skills.

In the future, this digital reputation may include more objective certifications for expertise in specific technical and soft-skill areas. The organization would identify the areas for certification (e.g., JavaScript, machine learning, user experience design). A process would then be developed to certify different levels of expertise. As we saw in chapter 5, Principle No. 3: Create a Learning Organization, this form of digital certification is a growing trend in the field of education.

Learning

Chapter 5 was dedicated to becoming a learning organization, so we won't spend a lot of time on this topic here. However, learning must be integrated as part of this new talent operating model. A talent platform delivers Inside Gig opportunities to learn by working with a new manager or a different set of peers with different backgrounds, doing the same type of work but in a different context, or just gaining exposure to something new and different. This type of learning builds better professionals because it affords employees a new perspective, broadens their understanding of the organization and helps them see the bigger picture.

The talent platform that facilitates this talent operating model uses AI capabilities to match individual skills, experiences, interests and aspirations with opportunities for growth. Therefore, it can also be linked to the organization's current learning management system (LMS), other internal training offerings, or other curated content the organization has a license to access (e.g., LinkedIn Learning, EdX, Coursera, Degreed, Udacity, Kahn Academy). By connecting these systems, an organization further embeds its goal of becoming a learning organization.

Career Advancement

It's a journey, not a ladder. If the organization moves away from traditional hierarchical structures and more toward networks of teams, the first question many will ask is: What about my promotion to X? We believe the term *promotion* should be replaced with *career progression*.

As we have seen, the delayering of organizations following the 2008 economic downturn resulted in flatter structures. Today's complex and evolving business environment means that the next career step is not necessarily always "up a ladder," but sometimes a lateral move across and into a new role with new, desired skill sets. It could mean a new role with greater impact or responsibility, but quite possibly an opportunity to expand into a new skill set that is strategic to the company. Thus career advancement is not about boxes on an organization chart, but rather about levels of education, experience, mastery of a subject and level of responsibility (which has to do with control over resources, both people and budget). The *only* aspect impacted by in the flattening of organization structures is less opportunity to increase people under management. However, there are other measures of responsibility, which may have to do with the size of projects you are managing.

But the shift to networks of teams makes the formal organizational structure less obvious. This is probably a good thing; it stops you from always looking at the job above and helps you think more about the journey you are on and where you want to go next. We promote the idea that a career is a journey, not a ladder that you climb; so let's take a journey together. Joe and Ivan may both start off in California and they might both end up in New York, but they might do it in different time frames and they certainly are likely to take different routes to get there. If Joe takes the northern route and Ivan takes the southern route, is one right and the other wrong? No, they each took the route that interested them the most.

That applies to a career as well. Two people who start in the same place almost always end up in different places. Similarly, people who start off in different places come together over time. There is no one right path. Today's world is so complex that it requires you to understand many different aspects of your business or discipline. The next step in your career is not always up; it is usually sideways to open new personal and professional opportunities. In fact, the next step in your career may not exist yet—but it will soon.

Inside gigs are ideal for exploring career options. An employee can take a small opportunity and try something new to see if it might interest them further. It just might be the next step in their career journey. Employees will know they are making progress in their journey because they are building new skills and learning to manage larger, more complex projects that are of growing importance to the company's mission. This is the real sign of career growth.

REWARDS AND COMPENSATION

When it comes to moving toward project-based work structures in general and leveraging this new talent operating model in particular, many questions get raised regarding compensation. In this section, we will first focus on rewards and recognition to encourage the adoption of this new talent operating model. Then we will address a shift in thinking regarding compensation as organizations begin to operate in this more agile approach to work.

Rewards

Strictly from a change management perspective, we have found it to be a best practice to provide some incentives to engage in this new way of working. For the most part, our interviews with companies experimenting with this type of talent operating model have indicated that employees are highly motivated to learn and grow and they want more choice in their work. Thus, no incentives should be necessary for them to participate in the process. However, if you are trying to foster a learning organization, it is possible to incentivize participating in the talent platform by giving participants access to more learning opportunities. This serves to reinforce what the Inside Gig offers to employees.

The most challenging shift required by this talent operating model is a mindset shift from scarcity of talent to abundance of talent. So we recommend that managers do need to have rewards and recognition tied to participation in this new way of working. For example, one manager behavior that should play a role in rewards is "providing employees with opportunities to leverage their skills and expand their capabilities on projects across the organization."

Compensation

As the world of work changes, so do the demands for how to compensate for a plurality of workers, types of work and methods for getting work done. A one-size-fits-all approach for employees with respect to compensation just won't work in this agile and evolving workforce. Three key tenets rise to the top for guiding compensation plans for the future:

1. Balance the stable versus the dynamic components of work.
2. Use a foundational framework to enable governance, agility and simplicity (manage against unintended outcomes).
3. Allow for personalization and customization (rethink rewards).[2]

Balance Stable vs. Dynamic Components of Work

Certain jobs in your work ecosystem may remain stable, while others may require new skills or change processes every six months. New skills are constantly on the horizon, some of which are critical to capitalize on in order to grow the business. It is essential to understand and track the skills needed in the organization, but it is illogical to try to pay for individual skills, as some of the skill-based pay programs of the past did. Skills often become obsolete quickly, and you certainly don't want to pay for something you don't need or use.

Developing an integrated work architecture—one that encompasses both a traditional job architecture (known and defined job families or disciplines) as well as an emerging work architecture (dynamic and evolving skills and knowledge)—will unlock the ability to describe the work that is stable and encompassed in a job as well as the work that is changing quickly. As described by John Bremen and Amy DeVylder Levanat in *Workspan* magazine, "Companies are aligning pay and responsibilities to more broadly defined roles that provide a platform for moving people between assignments, projects, departments and geographies."[3]

This allows more flexibility in getting the work done, building on core skills sets and avoiding the trap of having to constantly promote from narrowly defined job to job. Movement between roles may be based on an individual's skills and experience rather than their time in the role. A talent platform that supports this model will enable ease of tracking on both the supply side (What does our talent possess in terms of skills?) and the demand side (What skills are needed to get the work done?). By using the right foundational frameworks, pay can be appropriately attached to a variety of scenarios.

A Foundational Framework to Enable Governance, Agility and Stability

A streamlined approach to defining roles can be the key to paying appropriately and meeting the range of demands for governance and oversight. A simple leveling framework that utilizes work architecture and a streamlined set of levels will allow the definition of broader roles. Consider a role to be defined as the combination of job family or skill grouping level (e.g., contribution or capability) and type (e.g., management, individual contributor, sales, project manager). Aligning pay to roles allows flexibility for people to move between projects and assignments and utilize a broader range of skills within a cluster of skills (or skill family). An example can be drawn from one of the freelance talent platforms, such as Upwork. In the case of that platform, individuals pick a project that has been characterized based on level of expertise needed, skills needed and remuneration for the work. This is in essence a simple leveling framework that characterizes the work and aligns people to level and type of work needed as they sign up.

This provides a solid platform for differentiating pay by skill families where necessary. It also provides a method to conduct analytics to align with regulations around pay equity, hiring practices and so on. Some skills may demand higher rates in the market, and understanding the adjacencies between skills and creating broader skill families will ensure that organizations can align pay for roles appropriately without having to change pay rates for each and every skill. Movement between levels may be based on broad changes in scope and contribution; for some types of roles, particularly for individual contributor roles, it may be based on differences in capability (e.g., novice to expert). This approach allows the agility to continue to pay stable jobs that are the backbone of the organization using traditional pay components, while rethinking the pay approach for more dynamic, evolving skill families and roles.

Allow for Personalization and Customization (Rethink Rewards)

As skills and roles change, some organizations have begun to test a range of options for addressing both base and incentive pay. These options allow individuals to have more control over their remuneration, whether through choosing the type of role they want to work in, the types of skills they will learn, the next step in their career experience or which programs they choose to participate in. Some examples of these options include the following:

- Rethinking the purpose of base pay.

- Shifting from focusing on past performance to being more future focused. Salary adjustments are based on skills needed in the current role and skills that are critical to future success and perceived potential.

- Using more frequent salary adjustment periods (such as two times or four times a year).

- Managing the annual pay process in a more deliberate way, with different budgets to manage different aspects of pay—market competitiveness, pay equity, career progression—rather than one budget having to fit them all.

- Frequent spot bonuses to supplement and reward contribution.

- Giving a bonus to reward past performance, including the achievement of individual and team goals. This may involve paying a bonus for accomplishment of team goals upon project completion.

- Employing a range of reward options when an employee accepts an offer: a choice between an extra week of vacation or higher pay; higher bonus potential or more modest base pay increases.

- Employing a range of options that may lower overall costs (and thus increase spending power) such as volume discounts, childcare discounts or tuition reimbursement.

Regardless of how an organization chooses to approach compensation, one thing is clear—the factors that organizations rely on to determine base pay are changing (see Figure 10.1).

While past performance has traditionally been the biggest driver of base pay changes, having skills that are critical to the success of the current business strategy and remaining competitive for critical talent are two key issues in getting compensation right in the evolving world of work.

Figure 10.1 Getting Compensation Right

Posession of skills critical to the success of the future business model	51%
Concerns over market competitiveness	47%
Criticality of the role	34%
Percieved potential	31%
Achievement of team goals	30%
Addressing gender pay equality	28%
Demonstration of company values	25%
Achievement of individual goals	24%
Demonstration of knowledge and skills required in current role	22%
Concerns over internal equity	21%
Penetration in pay range for current role	21%
Final rating in most current year-end performance review	20%

Willis Towers Watson, *Getting Compensation Right Survey*, 2018.

These practices require the organization to have good information and employee analytics to understand trends in supply and demand for skills, costs and availability of skills in the market (internal and external), and tracking and achievement of team goals. Luckily, as the power of computing improves, data analytics and the use of analytics to support and drive human resource programs are moving from a dream to a reality.

KEY TAKEAWAYS

- New people capabilities will be needed to support the infrastructure of this talent operating model. This includes hiring a dedicated product manager to support the new process and technology implementation utilizing a communications platform tool to facilitate communications within and between teams.

- Each organization will need to create its rules of the road for deploying resources. While many organizations are leveraging the Inside Gig concept for development purposes only and assuming that employees have some slack time available to contribute to other projects while achieving their core job responsibilities, the Inside Gig talent operating model explicitly comes from a talent sharing perspective. Companies that adopt this approach have operated under the understanding that if an employee works on a project under a different cost center for under 20 percent of their time, budgets can accommodate these reallocations in resources (there is no change to budgets under these circumstances).

- Traditional processes assume hierarchical structures tied to specific jobs. Thus, talent management processes (e.g., performance management, learning, career advancement and compensation) need to be aligned to support this new way of working.

REFLECTION POINTS

If you are in a managerial role, how much independence do you think employees should have in applying for new projects?

Does your organization provide ongoing, continuous feedback from peers and managers to its employees, or would this be significant shift from how you manage performance today?

Are you leveraging technology to tie learning content to skill gaps?

In your view, how flexible is your organization in rethinking compensation and rewards with the rise of a new talent operating model?

CHAPTER 11
A New Talent Platform:
Taking an Idea from Concept to Action

What good is an idea if it remains an idea?
Try. Experiment. Iterate. Fail. Try again. Change the world.
—Simon Sinek

IN THIS CHAPTER, KELLEY PROVIDES a personal account of how the talent platform came to be. It is a story of *innovation to action,* and as Kelley will attest, you can't read *What Do You Do with an Idea?* by Kobi Yamada without walking away inspired. Who knew that among all of the business books, a children's book would ignite action? The spark is in the last line in Yamada's book: "And then, I realized what you do with an idea . . . You change the world."

FINDING LIKE MINDS AND CONNECTING DOTS

In early 2014, I got a phone call one day from a former colleague and mentor, Marianne Jackson. She was just stepping out of her role as CHRO at Blue Shield of California and was calling to tell me about a consortium of CHROs that had banded together called CHREATE. They were led by John Boudreau (professor, Management & Organization, Marshall School of Business, University of Southern California, and research director, Center for Effective Organizations, University of Southern California) and Ian Ziskin (president of EXcel Group

LLC and former CHRO of Northrop Grumman). Their objective was to start a movement to transform the HR function and enable the future of work.

Marianne knew that I had shown interest in this direction from our conversations over the years and my prior consulting assignment in the Innovation Management group at Genetech/Roche. She invited me to join her project team that would look at the forces of change affecting the landscape of HR. I was certainly interested in joining. So began my participation on a tiger team (a team of specialists in a particular field brought together to work on specific tasks) under Marianne in Phase I of CHREATE and, later, leading a project in Phase II within that same group. This inspiring experience helped cement my commitment to making a difference and propelling this movement in the HR profession. It turned out to be the start of several stars beginning to align. I would spend the next several years dedicated to the future of work.

The CHREATE group was made up of about 70 CHROs across multiple industries and some luminaries across human resources practice areas. We had one aim in common—to get our profession out of a rut and to start finding our way to create more value. We led many discussions about what we saw as threats to our profession and how we needed to disrupt the status quo or we'd find ourselves irrelevant. Many of the participants in this group could hardly ever be irrelevant—they were movers and shakers and the best of breed in our profession. In fact, it is where Edie Goldberg and I first reconnected, not yet knowing how closely we would soon partner together. I was humbled to be in the company of many of them, and I knew I would learn a lot just by being exposed to their experiences and their thinking.

Over the next two years, Edie and I worked with this group. The work over that time across multiple tiger teams resulted in an e-book, *Black Holes and White Spaces: Reimagining the Future of Work & HR with the CHREATE Project*,[1] and other learning materials. The group got together for a full day to share our collective learnings and the many products and resources that came out of the project. The results were quite astonishing. It was clear that we were on the road to making change happen. I recall presenting to the CHREATE group on the topic of The Rewiring of HR Tools and thinking, *I really need to do something with what I learned here.* The next week, I started white-boarding the concept of a platform for talent mobility.

After wrapping up the work with CHREATE, I decided to vet my thinking further. I had the fortune to be surrounded by brilliant people in my field and others who were giving me feedback on my crazy ideas. I began socializing the concept with experts in my network across academia, product development, engineering, HR and finance. To a person, it was clear that this idea had "legs"; a platform for talent mobility was a gap to be addressed. But finding time in a full-time role to truly develop the idea was going to be a challenge, and that's when good fortune found me: I was recruited to an organization that would soon be the best lab to bring this vision to reality and test its effectiveness.

A TALENT PLATFORM IS BORN

Into my world stepped Edzard Overbeek, a visionary and forward-thinking CEO who, in my opinion, "got HR." I recall our first interview in Los Altos, California, where we first discussed my vision for talent mobility. He had been thinking about how to build HERE Technologies, a global leader in mapping and location platform services, into an agile organization, and he immediately saw the benefits of a solution like I was describing. He made me an offer I couldn't refuse—come in-house as his chief human resources officer and he would fund a proof of concept (POC). Six months later, we assembled a small team of passionate software developers all over the world who believed in our vision, and we were off to the races.

Setting up the tiger team for the proof of concept would be the easy part; figuring out our own ways of working across the globe was a whole other challenge. We came together because of our passion, but not because we were geographically desirable. We decided quickly that we would use the methodology of the talent platform to build it—keep it small, break the work down into projects, keep our day jobs and devote a percentage of our time each week to getting this technology off the ground. Edzard gave us 10 weeks to deliver a POC, and we came through in 7½ weeks.

Taking It from Concept to Something Real

As a team, we got together and reviewed our objectives for this project and the technology:

1. Create a transparent technology that exposes the skills/capabilities of individuals that work in the company.

2. Create a talent marketplace for project-based work by organizational division that makes all work transparent such that that work can be effectively matched using ML/AI (machine learning/artificial intelligence) to skills in profiles system.

3. Create a beautiful UX/UI (user experience/user interface) environment and make it extremely intuitive and easy to use.

4. Run a pilot within two divisions to demonstrate a) the value of talent sharing across organizations; b) the opportunity to break organizational silos/build culture; c) the opportunity to create more learning opportunities; and d) the opportunity to automate the workflows to allow for choice. All with some checks and balances in place, of course.

With these objectives in mind, we set out to build the first prototype. We used a design-thinking approach to ensure that each frame of the talent platform was built with the user in mind. We conducted interviews across our stakeholder groups and ensured that each frame of the talent platform would achieve its intended purpose. We tested that first prototype and got positive, meaningful feedback, but we knew that without proper change management, the implementation of this technology and new way of working could fail. As a result, we sought some external help to build a change readiness assessment (CRA) while the team searched for two divisions that would want to pilot the technology (see Figure 11.1).

Figure 11.1 Change Readiness Assessment Framework

1 TALENT MINDSET

Perceptions and beliefs that shape performance behaviors

2 CULTURE

The behaviors that are expected, rewarded and discouraged on a recurring basis that influence performance outcomes

3 LARGE-SCALE CHANGE

The organization's history of large-scale change efforts; which ones succeeded, which ones failed and why

4 CURRENT TALENT OPERATING MODEL

The strategies, processes and methods used to acquire, develop, retain and deploy talent

Preparing for Seeds of Change

Knowing that we were embarking on a new way of operating, we expected resistance. So we contracted with two outside consultants, Edie Goldberg and Richard Mirabile. The first project was to build a CRA and the second was to define the new talent operating model that would support this new way of working. To start this process, we researched how other companies approached this challenge. Did they adopt a technology solution already in the marketplace, or did they build a custom solution to suit their own needs? We were interested in lessons for success and the learnings in any failed attempts. We wanted something to help us determine where to focus our change management efforts and to test our assumptions that leaders would likely resist our talent sharing approach at first. We figured other companies that had gone before us would be the best at helping us determine our path forward.

This is where I first directly worked with Edie and began to frame the beginnings of the new framework we would later refer to as the talent operating model. I sat down with Edie in early 2017 to engage her in helping me to define the model that supported my vision. From our initial benchmarking research, we had learned that other companies were building their own company-specific technology solutions to help them manage mobility in a way to drive better employee experiences. We concluded that there was clearly a gap in the market for a talent mobility solution and, so far, no one had the right technology solution or the best organizational framework to establish this new way of working.

We knew we had our work cut out for us, so we took those learnings and began to write a white paper to define what we heard and how we believed the future of work was calling for a new operating model. This new model would serve as a guide to companies on this journey. And in order to stand up this way of working, these organizations would need the right technology solution to enable it.

In parallel to our research and framing of the new talent operating model, we completed reviews of the CRA document and locked it down, then sent it out to sample group of leaders. The goal of the CRA was to quickly determine the hottest areas to focus on and mitigate the challenges. We sent the CRA to a sampling of leaders in the company and, as expected, the areas for greatest concern had to do with "leadership mindset." Given that the likelihood for success was highly dependent on leaders' support, we had to make a plan to not only address and mitigate leaders' concerns but to convert leaders to advocates. We knew this would take time and a concerted effort on communicating the "What's in it for me?" as a leader to get them over their objections.

So, you may be wondering how we addressed this issue with leaders. Our key strategy was to engage them directly by surfacing their fears. We held roundtables and yammer groups to dig deeply into their biggest fears for talent sharing across boundaries. It became clear that leaders were most worried about not getting work done successfully, a large concern because they were incentivized to meet goals and get their projects done. So we began to think through whether incentives were the right strategy (a more extrinsic approach) or whether we really needed to tie back to messaging on our core values. HERE Technologies had five company values and two of them specifically related to the effort—Give Back and Learn Fast. These core values illustrate how the giving/getting model would actually help them be recognized for getting more done. We drove the discussion around abundance versus scarcity and encouraged managers and leaders to try this new approach to getting work done and share feedback.

The result was truly amazing. As leaders who jumped in first started having success, those waiting on the sidelines started to get anxiety over a fear of missing out on something. We started to amplify the successes in our communications and videos. Employees began raving about managers allowing them to work on projects outside their home base, and before we knew it, the talent platform was becoming a vibrant marketplace. Engagement and productivity were on the rise, and the word on the street was "You'd better jump in." Our marketplaces were filling up with global, cross-functional opportunities, and with more successful projects coming to completion, the model for talent sharing started to germinate.

Starting Small

We started small by piloting the way of working first. It was a good strategy and one we now use with customers as they deploy this technology and way of working. We chose our two largest divisions in research and development (R&D), and we documented our successes and key learnings along the journey. We held postmortems with leaders who were posting opportunities, we road-tested our "rules" around the platform, and we leveraged the success of the pilot groups to seed the change with the rest of the organization. The pilot gave us an opportunity to test our users' experience and process flows and gave the tiger team on the platform a way to see the potential improvements as we took the solution enterprise-wide.

THE TECHNOLOGY ENABLED A NEW WAY OF WORKING

As we kicked off the enterprise deployment at HERE Technologies in June 2017, the original tiger team for the talent platform needed more resources. So we used the platform to post opportunities for UX/UI designer, communications, data science and other expertise. We were using the methodology behind the platform to build it. After all, we were facing similar constraints as our leaders were: we needed specific expertise and didn't have the headcount or budget for it. As a team, we started to experience the value in our own platform and notice areas needing improvement.

There were three key areas of the platform in our minimum viable product (MVP):

1. Profiles were based on skills, not simply experience.
2. The Marketplace for Projects was organized by functional units (e.g., Finance, Platform, Applications, COO). Later we added full-time opportunities to give a full view to work within the company.
3. Robust reporting (e.g., skill supply/demand, gaps, number of users, number of completed profiles).

Profiles Based on Skills

The novel aspect of our profiles is that, unlike LinkedIn profiles, they were created to market yourself internally. Your profile could be more personal and a place to showcase what you knew, but also what you aspired to learn. Because of this, we were able to use this data to dynamically match mentors and mentees based on specific learning objectives. Skills would be the foundation for how we managed work and learning. We made it easy to import data from other platforms such as LinkedIn, and included other relevant information about our employees like language fluency, experiences, hobbies and so on.

The Talent Marketplace

Part of the "What's in it for me?" for our employees to enter their profiles was the opportunity to participate in the project-based work
marketplace where they could be matched to assignments. We built the
platform with AI and ML and connected application programming
interfaces (APIs) to other collaboration software in our stack so that the
platform would reach out proactively to those employees who said they
had the skills required by that project. We set a simple set of rules and
programmed automation on manager workflows such that getting
invited or accepted into projects was easy for both *opportunity owners* (those
who were looking for services to get completed via the marketplace) and
opportunity seekers (those interested in participating in the projects). This
process was both a push and a pull. The system would reach out to
passive candidates through our collaboration platforms and scan all
possible matches. Opportunity owners could now tap into anyone in our
enterprise with a click of the button!

Although it took a while (approximately six weeks) for the marketplace
to take off, word spread quickly. With this new way of working, we were
starting to see savings, more cross-organization collaboration, employees
making new connections, and customer escalations handled more efficiently. The average time to find the right resource was within 24 hours.
Traditional recruiting methods could never have surfaced candidates
this quickly. In many cases, we were finding capacity in the organization
that helped us avoid hiring a contractor or opening a requisition. Work
was becoming democratized by giving employees choice in their work
assignments, and managers were getting more work done.

Data and Reporting

The platform was built for transparency. We didn't want a "Wizard of
Oz" behind the curtain manipulating data that wasn't available for all
users. There was some debate about this; however, we decided to hold
it as sacrosanct. If we were to be successful, we needed this platform
to be "for the people" and transparent. So, we embarked on what

reporting we would make available to users, and we landed on the following data in the beginning and knew this would evolve over time (see Figure 11.2). One critical element was to ensure the data were visual, making it easy to grab the insights quickly. Some data to adoption of the platform was for the tiger team, but all relevant data to our users was to be transparent. We continued to hone this reporting and believed that both opportunity owners and seekers would like to see information related to how this platform was being used.

Figure 11.2 Sample Reporting Template (for HERE Technology Platform)

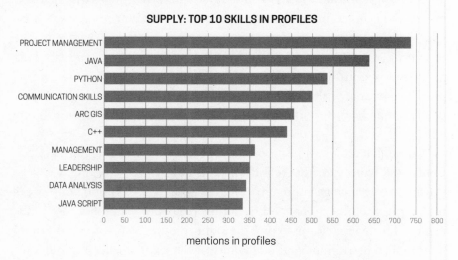

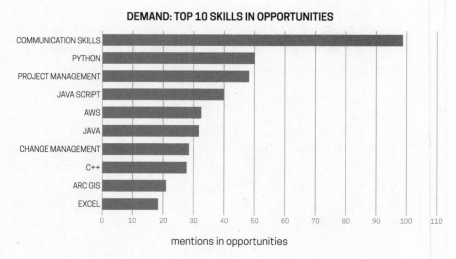

Figure 11.3 How Hitch Works

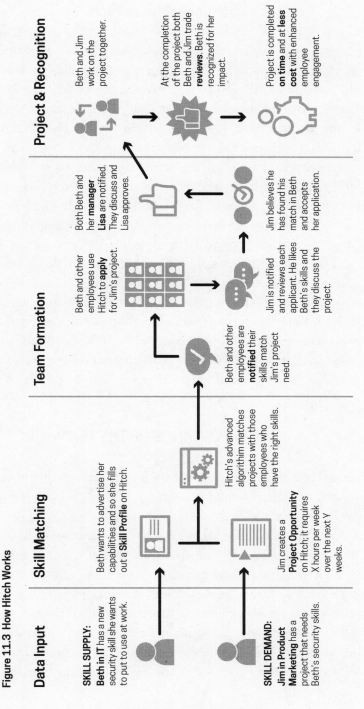

Putting It All Together

You may be wondering how the platform—which we came to call Hitch—worked in action. The premise is to quickly and accurately match in-demand skills with available supply by leveraging artificial intelligence and machine learning to find the right available talent to match the project or full-time work (see Figure 11.3 How Hitch Works).

In this example, Jim has a project that requires a high-demand skill set in security, and Beth, in the same organization, is looking for a way to leverage this new skill. Hitch is able to search through all the talent supply in the organization to find Beth for Jim's project. Jim is able to find Beth in seconds and reach out to her through the platform and invite her to his project. Beth is excited to demonstrate this new skill and make a contribution. Beth's manager is made aware through the automated system that Jim would like her to join, and she approves Beth's participation. Jim can now accept Beth onto the project and get started. Once the project wraps up, both Beth and Jim can trade reviews on each other and Jim "badges" Beth for her good work. Now everyone who sees Beth's project participation in her profile can also see the icon for "outstanding contribution" in her profile!

THE IMPORTANCE OF THE TEAM

People are central to this success story. The great experiment was to see how much human potential was unlocked when an environment was provided for people to make choices about their work, engage in something they were passionate about, and have the autonomy and opportunity to make an impact. I was simply an orchestra leader with a vision and a hope that, by putting the right elements together, we could successfully test this way of working. And we could show that a workplace that was based on abundance rather than scarcity, devoid of massive amounts of hierarchal management, and allowing some freedom of choice would not only avoid chaos but also create massive amounts of capacity and employee goodwill. If the goal was to transform the business and create a culture of performance, we were certainly on the right path.

Of all of the experiences and learnings that I had on this journey, probably the most important lesson to convey is this: Don't be afraid to try new models, to "tiptoe into the future of work." Your results might just surprise you. As I go out and talk about the future of work that I see, I am in good company. With talent shortages, disruption in business models and the rise of automation, those of us at the helm of driving outcomes through people need to take a hard look in the mirror and ask ourselves if we are innovating and experimenting enough. Are we taking the steps to ensure we are focused on building the workplace of the future? Can we sustain the tides of change with our current models, processes, technology and infrastructure? How can we ensure we are future-ready?

If you're asking yourself these questions, then you are already on the right path. It doesn't have to be scary or daunting. Edie and I encourage you to take the first step and you can read more details in the next two chapters to learn both through two case studies of companies implementing this new way of working as well as about the specific steps you can take into this new world of work. We hope you are as excited as we are to jump in and begin building the Inside Gig for your organization.

KEY TAKEAWAYS

- Never underestimate the power of the network you create and where you might find opportunity.

- Don't be afraid to try something new—whether a program, process or technology—and start small. You may learn more about the problem you intended to solve and those you didn't even knew you had when you started.

- People are dynamic and so capable of learning and growing beyond what they may have done to date—even *you!*

REFLECTION POINTS

Have you had a turning point in your life that has given you new insights into human potential?

Have you taken part in an initiative that has altered the way people work?

Do you have a mentor who has supported your professional growth?

Do you believe you have assets that would enable you to contribute more value to your organization?

PART FOUR
The Inside Gig in Action

One of the most important actions, things a leader can do,
is to lead by example. If you want everyone else to be passionate,
committed, dedicated, and motivated, you go first!
—Marshall Goldsmith

CHAPTER 12
Case Studies: HERE Technologies and Tata Communications

Do not go where the path may lead.
Go instead where there is no path and leave a trail. ·
—Ralph Waldo Emerson

IN THIS CHAPTER, WE DISCUSS CASE STUDIES of two companies that have, in different ways, implemented the Inside Gig. While this is a very new way to manage talent within the organization, these two companies are by no means the only ones experimenting with this type of fluid talent mobility. We are aware of other innovative companies (such as Dolby, Patagonia, IBM, Cisco Systems, eBay, Accenture and Unilever) that are implementing similar approaches to moving talent around the organization to better leverage their skills and facilitate learning and innovation. The case studies here are intended to help further articulate why companies are choosing to change the way in which they work, how they are approaching this change, what the keys to success have been for each company, and how they have measured their impact.

CASE STUDY 1: HERE TECHNOLOGIES

AN OVERVIEW OF HERE TECHNOLOGIES

HERE Technologies has more than 9,200 employees and operates in more than 50 countries around the world. Over 30 years ago, HERE began with the goal of digitizing mapping and pioneering in-car navigation systems. Over the next three decades, HERE built a legacy in mapping technology. Today, HERE is creating three-dimensional maps with layers of information and insights. And the company is looking beyond mapping to autonomous driving, the Internet of Things, and building the future of location technology through strategic partnerships. At the core of the strategy is building open solutions for the future and, as they say in their vision, "Enabling an Autonomous World for everyone."

It is HERE's ambition to be a great place to work where employees thrive in their careers, develop their skills and can make major contributions to the company. This required adopting new mindsets, shifting cultural norms and implementing a new talent operating model. CEO Edzard Overbeek has been with the company for more than four years and is quite ambitious about the possibilities that HERE is building a digital representation of reality entirely built upon location data and become a leading platform company centered on location intelligence. He clearly articulated with his most senior leadership that the challenge in realizing his vision required a change not only in the business model and the talent composition, but also in breaking traditional ways of working.

THE BUSINESS CASE

Meeting the high ambitions to become a platform company required that HERE transform itself in all aspects of the business: the business model, product, operations and leadership, and workforce skills and capabilities. The company was traditionally based in content for maps and faced a commoditization of the business. There was clearly a case for change; HERE was competing with some of the largest and most powerful technology companies in the world.

HERE strived to become an integrated platform company. Integrated platforms are so called because they enable participants to create value in two ways: they offer technologies or data as building blocks that others can use to develop their own products or services (a service platform), and they facilitate interactions between individuals or organizations that would otherwise have difficulty finding each other (a marketplace).

Leading a company going through this type of major transformation required a new type of leadership. Edzard was chosen by the board as he exemplified the capabilities required to drive change. Edzard spent the better part of his career breaking barriers and finding new approaches. His visionary approach and charisma made him an exemplary CEO to lead HERE Technologies through this massive transformation in the business. His willingness to break traditional business models and disrupt the status quo inspired employees to buy into his vision of success.

Shortly after Edzard was hired, he began building out his leadership team, including hiring Kelley Steven-Waiss as his new chief HR executive. To facilitate the transformation of the organization, the leadership team wanted to address both the company culture and people practices. Thus, together with Kelley, the leadership team created a three- to five-year road map of a people strategy that would define the shifts that the organization needed to make.

To have an accurate understanding of what that cultural transformation should entail, it was important to get a baseline on the culture from the employees' perspective. And the results from the first HERE culture audit illustrated that there was organizational inertia due to an unclear company vision, a lack of urgency around changes needed in the business, and a workforce that wasn't galvanized around a common strategy or core values. The first priority related to the people strategy was to tackle the culture change head on. Norms and values were redefined so that employees could rally behind them and they could be carefully embedded in all of the programs and ways of working.

But culture changes do not occur simply because leadership defines and communicates a new set of cultural norms. A change management approach is needed. The HR team decided to offer employees options for a new set of core values and allow them to take ownership of those values by determining which ones resonated and how to define them. This created the guiding coalition for the change efforts and employees who had skin in the game to adopt and model the behaviors.

SETTING THE CHANGE AGENDA:
THE HERE TECHNOLOGIES PEOPLE STRATEGY

Figure 12.1 HERE Technology's People Strategy Pillars

3 pillars—people strategy (2019)

Support HERE's transformation to a high-performance organization and platform company through the design and delivery of people practices, policies and programs that enable global talent mobility, operational excellence and scalability, and a one HERE culture, i.e., "the HERE way"

Global Talent Mobility	Operational Excellence	One HERE
Deliver a **world-class global workforce** by attracting, deploying, developing and retaining our critical capabilities.	Design and execute **processes, tools and people practices** that support transformation and scalability to enable people to do their best work.	Build an **inclusive culture** on the foundation of our core values that drives **innovation, productivity and engagement.**

The gaps identified between HERE's aspirations and its current culture called for a method for greater talent mobility, higher levels of operational excellence and automation of tools, and a common culture that redefined what it meant to be a HERE employee no matter where your office was around the world. As such, the HERE 3-Year People Strategy (2016–2019) (see Figure 12.1) focused on three major pillars that would be further defined into all HR objectives and would address the following "pains" and "gains."

PAINS
- Lack of talent visibility (skills supply chain)
- Employees working in silos; lack of internal mobility
- Limited development and learning opportunities
- Low levels of employee engagement

GAINS
- Enhance productivity and accelerate innovation
- Manage the skill gap between supply and demand
- Upskill and reskill the workforce, where necessary
- Increase employee engagement
- Deploy agile teams with speed and efficiency

GETTING STARTED:
HOW HERE TECHNOLOGIES IMPLEMENTED THE INSIDE GIG

With a major focus on talent mobility, the organization needed to determine how best to facilitate the movement of employees in a highly complex, global environment. The HR systems at HERE were not designed to identify or quantify workforce skills, so the company had to develop a technology that would allow for an accurate view of each employee's current skills profile. This would not be a simple task. HERE operates in highly regulated environments with respect to individual privacy, and employees may be reluctant to voluntarily share their skills if there is no perceived exchange of value to them. The team addressed this issue by creating two workstreams: 1) to build a technology platform to facilitate the process; and 2) to work through any necessary change management or operating model shifts that would be needed to embed this new way of working in the company culture.

Implementing the Talent Platform—Hitch
The HERE Talent Platform, later known as Hitch, became the technology enabler used to create an internal talent marketplace. Using machine learning and artificial intelligence to map skills to work, the platform enabled a project-based or agile work environment. But it wasn't without challenges or learnings along the way. Creating a new way of working felt, at times, like swimming upstream. Changing

what is comfortable and familiar for employees was not going to occur without cultural hurdles. A simple aspiration to change was only the first step.

The Talent Operating Model Shift

Given that leaders and people managers needed to support talent sharing across organizational boundaries, there had to be a focus on these stakeholders and the potential for roadblocks. After establishing the vision of where we wanted to go and getting support from the C-suite, we ran a change readiness assessment to determine what areas would be of greatest concern. The results of that assessment illustrated to us that our biggest challenge was going to be getting senior leaders to believe that sharing talent would not create issues for them in getting the work accomplished for which they had greatest accountability. The HERE team had to demonstrate that by accepting the "abundance view" rather than the "scarcity view," senior leaders and people managers would have an opportunity to get *more* accomplished, even if that meant sharing talent outside of their functional areas.

Starting Small The HERE Talent Platform team, in partnership with HR business partners and communicators, created a change strategy that began with a pilot. We agreed that we would not make participation mandatory, and that we would allow for more organic participation and demonstrate the value of talent sharing by starting with two business units in the pilot. It was further decided that both of these business units had to meet the following criteria:

1. Each business unit needed to have a global talent base or operate in at least two different regions.
2. Each business unit had to have project-based work that would require similar talent or skills and be willing to share the full-time equivalent (FTE) with the other business unit.
3. Each business unit would need an actively engaged group of senior leaders and people managers willing to try this new way of working and give feedback on their results, including capturing success stories.
4. Each business until would not offer additional compensation or awards for talent sharing; however, they would recognize employees or managers who participated.

The pilot kicked off with training the people managers or opportunity owners on how to break the traditional FTE roles into projects or work that based on services and skills. The pilot ran for 90 days. The team reconvened at the end to review results and challenges, and to determine if and how the company should roll out this way of working further.

Company-Wide Rollout After the 90 days were completed, the team did a post-pilot review and found instances where talent sharing was making a positive impact in the following ways:

1. Talent was being shared across business units with minimal to no disruption to existing work.
2. Work was not only cross-functional, but global; teams were forming across traditional company silos.
3. Project opportunities were being posted more often by "new users," and adoption was increasing each week.
4. Users (both people managers or opportunity owners and participants) were being matched to work, at times, within 24 hours.

The pilot was so successful that the CEO and his leadership team decided in June 2017 to roll out the platform company-wide.

Keys to Success
The HERE team would advise any organization wishing to embark on this way of working to follow these actions, which they believe to be key to HERE's success:

1. Execute a change readiness assessment and build a change management plan that addresses the challenges for your culture.
2. Start with a pilot program before rolling it out to the rest of the company, with clear metrics or key performance indicators about what success looks like.
4. Embed talent mobility into the people or talent strategy of your organization; tie this directly to your organization's cultural values.
5. Utilize the early adopters (both senior leaders/managers and participants) to role-model this way of working.

6. Create talent platform "champions" to act as ambassadors for the program.

7. Communicate and celebrate the success of this way of working by sharing the stories internally.

Results to Date

After the first year after launching the Hitch platform and embedding this way of working, the company has posted some amazing results, including over 111 FTEs worth of work performed that would have otherwise been outsourced or hired from the outside, and over 600 projects completed in the platform.

Figure 12.2 Hitch: Results over First Year

Productivity

FTE worth of capacity
111 FTE
Completed

Engagement

HERE Promoter Score increased 9% over the last 12 months

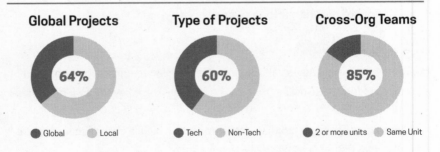

Global Projects	Type of Projects	Cross-Org Teams
64%	60%	85%
● Global ○ Local	● Tech ○ Non-Tech	● 2 or more units ○ Same Unit

"When in need for skills, capabilities and experience we often tend to look for it outside the company as a first option because we don't have the visibility to the existing talent. With the talent platform we created a unique and continued insight in all of our internal talent and were able to dynamically mobilize it to solve our toughest challenges while in parallel creating new and exciting opportunities for our people."
— Edzard Overbeek, CEO of HERE Technologies

HERE senior leaders and employees adopted this new way of working and see it as a central part of the transformation of the business. Although it wasn't without challenges, the move to project-based work and an agile work environment will continue to be a pivotal part of HERE's strategy to evolve into the leading open location platform company.

A Leader's View

Emmanuel Arbogast, HERE Project Leader, on the Effectiveness of Hitch

Often Hitch is used for short-term projects that require a portion of employees' time. The Open Location Platform (OLP) Analytics team identified data scientists as ideal users of the OLP, so the team members decided to create an OLP Software Development Kit (SDK) for data scientists in Python, their preferred programming language. However, a crucial problem quickly became apparent: the OLP Analytics team was primarily made up of Java and Scala experts, the primary languages for most OLP users, but not Python.

With no expertise on the team, no idea where to find Python expertise internally, and no time to recruit Python expertise externally, Emmanuel Arbogast, the project leader, described the situation as a "nightmare." To address the skill gap, Emmanuel turned to Hitch, HERE's new talent platform. In minutes, a few experts within HERE applied for the opportunity to join the project team. "We hadn't even finished the meeting where we set up the Hitch opportunity before we started receiving applications," Emmanuel said.

Fast mobilization of untapped skills is what Hitch does best. It bootstrapped a project for a team that didn't otherwise have the skills to execute it. But thanks to Hitch, the OLP Python SDK project began on time and with new, deep expertise on board. Six HERE colleagues from Berlin, Eindhoven, Burlington and Seattle—all with Python expertise—collaborated on this project. They committed a minimum of 20 percent of their time. And a few of them devoted 100 percent of their time to the project because they—and their managers—saw the customer value in developing an OLP Python SDK. Emmanuel summed up the experience by saying, "The ability to borrow skills within HERE afforded us the time to upskill the existing team while still meeting project deadlines. It's very clear to me that this project would not be off the ground today without Hitch."

CASE STUDY 2: TATA COMMUNICATIONS

AN OVERVIEW OF TATA COMMUNICATIONS

Tata Communications Ltd. was incorporated in 1986 in India. It is the leading provider of network, cloud, mobility, collaboration and security services. This approximately $2.4-billion company has more than 11,500 employees operating out of 14 countries, with presence in over 200 countries and territories around the world. Tata Communications' purpose is to facilitate transformation for positive change for everyone. Its fiber network carries approximately 30 percent of the world's Internet routes, connecting four out of five mobile subscribers worldwide.

THE BUSINESS CASE

Tata Communications built its Inside Gig talent platform in response to both external factors and internal issues the company needed to address. Employees wanted more choice and personalization of their work experience, as they were becoming accustomed to consumer-grade applications such as Airbnb, Uber and Facebook that created personalized experiences. The company observed how technology was disrupting industries and how artificial intelligence was being used to automate many processes. In addition, as Tata Communications expanded globally, it had to not only conform to local expectations, but also be more responsive to global trends.

Internally, the company wanted to reduce its very high staffing cost base, as costs were outpacing revenues. The telecommunications industry, including Tata Communications, was beginning to see a massive shift in skill obsolescence; the digital transformation was impacting every aspect of the business. While the company knew that a big shift in skills would be needed across the organization, it did not know which specific skills would be needed and what the demand would be. The traditional approach to developing talent was not growing the capabilities the company needed at the pace it needed, so it was constantly buying skills (hiring externally) at a high cost. The company recognized the need to become a learning organization so that it could grow the skills needed for the future. Further, it needed to change its ways of working to do a better job of leveraging latent skills and potential in the organization. Innovation could be increased by creating more cross-boundary collaborations to expand the thinking and approach to new problems.

Tata Communications believed this was a problem worth solving. Its business was moving from being a traditional telecom company to becoming a new age digital infrastructure provider to serve their customers in the digital economy. Aadesh Goyal, Tata Communications global chief human resources officer, said he "wanted to create a smart ecosystem to run [the] business."

HOW TATA COMMUNICATIONS IMPLEMENTED THE INSIDE GIG: THE PROJECT MARKETPLACE

The solution developed to respond to the business challenges was called the Project Marketplace. Tata Communications looked to the external market for a technology solution that would facilitate this process, but none existed. As a result, the company decided to create its own system by linking together systems it already used (SharePoint, Azure, SuccessFactors, HRMS, Skype, Outlook and Yammer). Through API integrations, Tata Communications was able to create an infrastructure that supported its needs, without building everything from scratch.

The company approached its new talent infrastructure with a design-thinking philosophy. A product manager was put in charge of creating a consumer-grade platform. The result was a minimum viable product offered to the workforce on a voluntary basis. The team monitored behavior and analytics to inform design decisions through experimentation with different options. After two and a half years of use, the company has a process it is comfortable with, but continues to monitor and adapt to improve.

To build a database of employee skills, employees completed surveys and identi-fied their skills, which would allow them access to projects in the Project Marketplace.

Tata Communications incentivized employees to be early adopters and gamified the system by awarding points to encourage employees to update their skills.

Using technology and design thinking, Tata Communications has developed a talent platform in-house that has created a freelance skill delivery network within the organization, mirroring the external gig economy.

A project manager in need of skills can post a project to the Project Marketplace (see Figure 12.3 Tata Communications' Project Marketplace Process). When doing so, the project manager must identify the skills needed and determine the scope and duration of the project. The system uses artificial intelligence to match an employee to the opportunity, regardless of the employee's current job title or department. The manager gets a curated list of resources with links to those employee skill profiles and their availability. Employees who have signed up with the Project Marketplace also get notified when their skills match an opportunity. So it is a two-way communication system. Ultimately, project managers get to choose the team they want. Then, the project manager and employee jointly agree on scope, deliverables and the timeline.

Figure 12.3: Tata Communications' Project Marketplace

POST A PROJECT
Scope, duration, skills needed

SHORTLISTED RESOURCES
Review skills, profile, availability

INDUCT
Agree on scope, deliverables and timelines

COLLABORATE
Chat, share files and share feedback on your own workplace

FEEDBACK
Rate the team member to provide a rating through Insta applause

Identify a wide range of talent and resources across the globe

More cost-effective than hiring consultants/ contractors

Build networks and be a mentor, coach and guide

Extended team with just-in-time access to the required skils

Tata Communications, 2019.

In addition to posting an opportunity and letting the system match employees to projects, the system also allows managers to search for specific skill sets to find out where that talent exists within the company. The Skills Warehouse groups people with similar skills to help those people form a community. Skill communities may reach out to each other for learning and collaboration. This is another way the talent platform enables a learning organization.

The focus of the Project Marketplace is on skill development, and it is completely voluntary. The company does not use the principle "You get what you give"; employees are not released from any of their job responsibilities. They can apply for as many projects as they like. Only their skills and bandwidth limit their ability to take on a new project. However, business-as-usual deliverables remain sacrosanct. They must deliver on their day-to-day job.

In the two and a half years that the Project Marketplace has been in operation, there has never been a conflict with an employee not delivering on their core job because they were taking on other work in the Project Marketplace. However, because participating in the Project Marketplace is voluntary, and employees remain responsible for meeting their day-to-day responsibilities, only a small percentage of the company's employees have the time or take the initiative to participate in the talent platform.

The company uses existing social collaboration tools to aid employees in working together on projects. When a project is completed, both the project manager and team members provide a rating and feedback in these areas:

- Overall contribution to the project
- Skills used in the project
- Execution of the project benchmarked against company values

This feedback adds to the employee's skills profile and helps them to develop an internal reputation.

The Talent Operating Model Shift

Tata Communications' first step in implementing the Project Marketplace was to clearly define the new ways of working, or what it called the "rules of the game." The rules were meant to provide more power to the employee to democratize work within a voluntary system. Employees were held personally accountable for delivering on both their day-to-day job responsibilities and their Project Market-place commitments. Because employees had personal accountability, the process required no approvals from a manager to allow their employees to work on other projects. Project managers were given full authority to select whomever they wanted on their team (no oversight), although the system helped those managers identify the best-matched talent. That talent could come from anywhere, so it helped to break down silos across the organization.

To support this new approach to work and reinforce the desire to become a continuous learning organization that could build its own talent within, the company has embarked on a series of changes to the talent management systems, which create a mutually supporting system to enable employees to manage their life and work. Here are a few of the talent management processes that support, or are supported by, the Talent Marketplace.

Flexibility at Work and Life Event Assistance Program (LEAP) Tata Communications has received public recognition for its leading stance on supporting working parents. The company offers six months of paid leave for the primary caregiver of a newborn (irrespective of gender). The secondary caregiver is also provided two weeks of paid leave. The Project Marketplace is one element of LEAP through which employees can engage in short-term projects while away on caregiver leave, if desired by the employee. It also provides a way for them to transition back to a full-time role more slowly by taking on projects, rather than coming directly back to their job. In early 2019, the company launched a new policy that allows employ-ees with six months of tenure to choose their number of working hours in order to help them create more work-life balance.

Winning Mix In 2014, Tata Communications set internal goals for increasing the number of women in their company, with the belief that a better balance of men and women would create a winning mix of ideas and perspectives. When the initia-tive began, women made up only 15 percent of the company's workforce. Today, after almost doubling their employee population, 23 percent of the workforce population is female. Platforms such as the Project Marketplace, alongside the policies described above, create a culture and a context that attracts and retains talent.

Learning and Development Three years ago, 90 percent of training offered by the company was classroom-style training and 10 percent was digital (online). Today, this has shifted to 80 percent digital content complemented by 20 percent classroom training. Flexible on-demand access to training is needed to support individuals working in the Project Marketplace (and elsewhere in the organization). With the changing nature of work, this organization is acutely aware of the need to reskill its employees. Offering bite-size learning opportunities, as well as on-demand content, the company modernized its approach to learning to fit its employees' needs.

Tata Communications has linked its internal skills frameworks to internal and external curated content, which points employees to the training that will help to advance specific, desired skills. The gamification of the talent platform (winning points for updating your profile, completing a project and completing feedback reviews on peers) earns employees credits to external learning experiences (on-demand courses, attending conferences and certification) that they value for their careers. With the shift to more digital learning solutions and new ways for employees to earn access to special development opportunities, the average number of training days per employee has doubled.

Action Learning Platform The organization has identified the critical skills it needs for the future, but these skills are not available in the organization today, neither in general capability nor in the capacity they will need moving forward. The company is using the Project Marketplace to facilitate a skills transformation within the company. Specifically, it is leveraging its external freelance network to bring in experts to the Project Marketplace to lead action learning projects to transfer skills to their employees.

Keys to Success

Leaders at Tata Communications would point to three elements that have enabled the success of the Project Marketplace:

1. **Leveraging networks:** When an employee joins the network, the system reaches out to the employee's connections and encourages the employee's friends to join. For example, when John joins the network, his peer Kate gets a note saying, "John just started an assignment on the Project Marketplace.

Ask him about it and learn how this can benefit you and your career."
The system also provides prewritten invitations that employees working on
the platform can use to invite their friends to join. Employees earn points as
an incentive for inviting friends.

2. **Gamification:** Tata Communications integrated its recognition platform with
the Project Marketplace and created a scoreboard where employees could
advance through six levels to earn or redeem points for learning experiences.
Points can be earned by activities such as updating your profile, inviting peers
to join the platform, applying for projects, completing projects and so on.

3. **Storytelling:** There's nothing like a good story to create pull for a new process.
The company curated success stories of employees who were able to work
on projects outside of their normal team to develop new skills that led to
new career opportunities. The company also shared stories from project
managers who were quickly able to address problems by rapidly pulling
together a team. Other stories focused on how employees were able to put
to use skills they have that were underutilized in their current role, allowing
them to have greater impact.

Results to Date

The Project Marketplace was launched in November 2016. The number of projects
completed and employees engaged is one way to measure success, but Tata
Communications is more focused on the long-term impact of this new, more
democratized way of distributing work. The company believes it will change the
fabric of the company by creating a learning culture. The real value is from the
work that gets done and the projects the company is able to win or successfully
execute because it has the right talent in the right place at the right time. Three
years ago, when this process was launched, the organization had serious concerns
about the talent risks it faced due to the changing skill sets required by the digital
revolution. Today, the company has significantly fewer concerns because it has
created an infrastructure to build its own talent.

Project Marketplace metrics tracked include the following:

- 13,000 visitors since launch
- 175 projects posted globally
- 800 employees who have worked on projects of their choice

- 2,000 people engaged—whether they have created a profile, referred a friend, applied for a job or completed projects—through the gamification of the platform

KEY TAKEAWAYS

- Creating an Inside Gig opportunity platform gives organizations an opportunity to personalize the employee experience at work.

- The talent operating model for the Inside Gig doesn't require a lot of management oversight or administration. In the case studies presented in this chapter, neither company was required to create a lot of rules. Instead, the companies were guided by principles and sought to democratize the work, or give employees more choice in the projects they participated in.

- While we promote a "You get what you give" approach to work, where time for inside gigs are carved out of an employee's normal work week, some companies offer inside gigs on top of the day-to-day work. However, there is a significant difference in the uptake of learning opportunities when they are layered on top of regular job responsibilities.

- Start small and pilot the process in parts of the organization that will be most open to this type of change. Learn from the pilot and adapt.

- You'll have a greater chance of embedding this way of working if part of the organization's greater people strategy and practices are aligned to support this new approach to work.

- Storytelling is an important change management technique to reinforce the change and reference the successes.

- When rolling out the technology and the way of working, establish key performance indicators for success, and evaluate areas for improvement or where more change management is required.

REFLECTION POINTS

Do you think your organization will consider experimenting with the types of fluid talent mobility presented in the case studies?

What struck you as the primary hurdles that needed to be overcome by HERE Technologies and Tata Communications in building their talent platforms?

How would you assess the alignment of leadership with embedding new ways of working in your organization?

As you reflect on the preceding chapters and these two case studies, what new approaches to work are you interested in experimenting with? How do you plan to get started?

CHAPTER 13
Taking the First Step

The discipline of writing something down
is the first step toward making it happen.
—Lee Iacocca

I<small>T'S A DAUNTING TASK TO CREATE</small> fluid work experiences that enable the organization to become more agile. But consider that traditional approaches to work (stable jobs and hierarchical reporting structures) have been with us for over a century. We hope that we have created a compelling case to consider using the Inside Gig talent operating model and have helped you to understand the core principles that underpin this new way of working. The first step is always the hardest. In this chapter, we share how other companies have taken the first step on this path, as well as lessons learned about creating a foundation for success.

BUILD THE BUSINESS CASE FOR CHANGE

Part One of this book, The Time for the Inside Gig Has Come, provides an overview of the research a company needs to establish a strong business case for making changes within an organization. While each organization must augment the business case we provided with facts from its own business context (e.g., turnover rates, increasing skill obsolescence, shifts in business strategy), you need to start by selling the concept to the leadership team. The business case must support the need for a mindset shift from one of talent scarcity to one of abundance of talent. Admittedly, this is a huge shift in how a company thinks about talent. We know that change is hard and that resistance is the norm. However, the benefits of embracing this new way of working far outweigh the benefits of staying with comfortable old habits. Improvements in productivity and employee engagement, cost savings, and the ability to innovate are just some of the demonstrated benefits of this new approach. The status quo may, in time, lead to business failure.

Once the leadership team agrees to the concept of the Inside Gig, the team also needs to embrace the need to shift the talent operating model. The size of such a shift will differ for each company based on its current operating model (its ways of working, and alignment of HR policies and processes to support this change). For some companies that already operate in a project-based work system, it may be a minor pivot. For other companies where it is a significant change, we recommend taking small progressive steps.

ASSESS ORGANIZATIONAL READINESS

To figure out if your organization is ready to take on this type of change, and to assess what will be the biggest barriers to success, we recommend completing a change readiness assessment. This type of assessment examines the organization along four dimensions: 1) mindset; 2) culture; 3) change management; and 4) alignment of the talent operating model, with a specific emphasis on current talent processes.

As we discussed earlier, in particular in chapter 3, Principle No. 1: You Get What You Give, the shift in mindset is the most challenging to overcome. It is important to understand the current mindset of your managers to know how much of a shift you need to manage to implement the Inside Gig. Some topics you might assess related to mindset include the following:

1. Do managers operate from a scarcity of talent mindset, where they hoard talent because they are afraid to give up even one-tenth of a resource?

2. Do managers only think of their employees in terms of the skills they bring to their immediate job or task, or do they consider the wealth of experiences employees may bring with them from their past or current interests outside of work?

3. Do managers operate from a growth mindset rather than a fixed mindset (as discussed in chapter 5, Principle No. 3: Create a Learning Organization)? That is, do they believe that their employees can learn, grow and improve, or do they view employees as static beings, who are unable to grow their knowledge or expertise?

As discussed in chapter 9, A New Talent Operating Model: Rethinking Ways of Working, many aspects of your company culture can support this type of change. Here are some questions that tap into this dimension:

- Does the organization value accomplishment over authority, or does hierarchy largely determine the role people play in projects (i.e., who is a participant and who is a leader)?

- Do you operate in an agile and boundaryless manner with lots of cross-functional collaboration, or is there a strong internal commitment to the function an employee belongs to, leading to a silo mentality?

- Does your organization encourage employees to challenge the status quo, or do you abide by a philosophy of "If it ain't broke, don't fix it"?

- Do managers value diversity of thought, or are teams likely to resemble their leader in terms of demographics, expertise, past experience, education and so on?

- Do managers spend more time managing the organization's politics than they do looking for optimal solutions for the company?

- Are employees encouraged to contribute to the team based on the skills they were hired for, or are they encouraged to follow their passion?

All of these cultural characteristics will help you to understand where your points of resistance may come from when implementing the Inside Gig. With this assessment, an organization can craft specific strategies to shift the culture.

In order to not repeat past failures, it's helpful to understand the company's history with implementing large-scale change. That includes manager and employee perceptions regarding how well the organization communicates about forthcoming change. If there are bottlenecks in communications (e.g., are middle managers a pinch point for information flow?), identify this from the outset so that specific strategies can be developed to do better than past unsuccessful implementation efforts. It goes without saying that the misalignment of strategy and structure will lead to unsuccessful outcomes.

Be sure to identify where conflicts lie between the current talent operating model and the talent operating model that drives the Inside Gig. For example, does the organization currently operate with a distributed decision-making ethos, or are decisions made at the top and communicated down through the organization? Does the organization select candidates for organizational fit, or are skills and experience for the role the only consideration? Are learning and development programs compliance-focused, or are they geared toward ongoing individual growth? Does the organization recognize and reward managers for the development of their employees, or are managers only recognized for business results? Is the performance management process a traditional annual process where only the manager's input is deemed important, or is feedback more ongoing or project-based, with inputs from others with whom the employee interacts?

Armed with information on how the company operates today, you can assess if there is a high level of readiness for change because

a) the organization has solid change management practices in place, and b) the culture of the organization and mindset of managers are more aligned with than opposed to the principles of the Inside Gig. If there are significant barriers to success, you may be wise to start small by developing strong change management practices and taking some interim steps to change the culture, and aligning some talent management practices to support this new way of working.

DO YOU BUILD OR BUY TECHNOLOGY TO ENABLE THE PROCESS?

When we first came up with the idea of being able to fully leverage the talent within the organization and create a new way of working that supported a continuous learning organization, there was no technology on the marketplace to facilitate such a process. Every company we spoke to that was experimenting with working in this manner had custom-built its own internal platform. If you are a large technology-based organization, this approach may work. But thankfully for the rest of the business world, access to technology has now gotten easier.

Over the past three years, we have seen a dramatic rise in the perceived importance of working in this more agile manner and a desire to help employees connect for personal growth. This interest has led to the development of some new technologies that aid in executing against this process. Hitch (which you will be familiar with from chapters 11 and 12) and Gloat are two of the newest products on the market that enable the Inside Gig approach to talent mobility. Other technologies such as Fuel50 and Bridge are more focused on career development than on short-term internal talent mobility; however, companies have been leveraging them for similar goals. Other technologies are likely to arise in the near term. Whichever path an organization decides to take, big data and machine learning can aid these new solutions. This new way of working is way too complex to do without the support of a robust technology. So, buy it or build it—but you will need technology to enable the process to work.

DEFINE THE NEW WAYS OF WORKING: RULES FOR THE ROAD

We chose to open this chapter with the quote from Lee Iacocca because once an organization has management buy-in for the change, and once you understand the change readiness of the organization, then the next step is to clearly define the new ways of working. Start by writing it down. Create rules of the road for your managers and employees to follow, so they understand what is expected of them to work in this new manner.

It's necessary to gain alignment from senior management on the desired culture or on how this new way of working will further reinforce the existent culture. New behavioral expectations for leaders must be made very clear. We suspect that if a company already has clearly defined leadership behaviors, some modifications will be needed to support this way of working. For example, the expectation that leaders must develop their employees is not a common one in most organizations. However, organizations today are also operating at a much more rapid pace of change.

While the new ways of working may require some changes to organizational structures (e.g., governance structures that will address significant cross-functional business decisions, such as setting up a project management office), pushing decision-making down to the team level requires a clear articulation about the parameters within which teams can make decisions on their own, without seeking input or approval from higher levels within the company.

Every organization we have spoken to about this approach to work has made it voluntary for their employees. No one is forced to take part in a project outside of their regular role. Other rules of the road may hit on topics such as these:

- Who is allowed to post projects: any employee? only managers?

- Who is allowed to apply for projects: any employee? only those who are not on a performance improvement plan? both employees and external freelancers?

- What type of information is required when posting an opportunity (e.g., skills needed, skill level, time commitment, duration of project, physical location or remote work)?

• How does selection onto a project happen?

• Do employees apply for a project or are they recruited? Are they matched or do they have to proactively search, or both?

• Do you need to notify your current manager? If so, at what stage of the process?

• Is there a limit to the amount of time a person can work on projects outside of their regular job?

Another issue that must be proactively addressed is how the role of a manager is defined in this new way of working. If an employee may work with multiple project managers, how will those individuals provide input on the employee's performance and potential? As described in chapter 7, Principle No. 5: Create an Agile Organization, it may be time to rethink the role of the manager and create two separate roles: the project leader and career coach.

While we recommend that you create some rules of the road, it isn't necessary to be overly prescriptive. This is a new way of working in a very agile manner. If you are operating in an agile environment, you should test and iterate. As George Hudgens from Dolby Laboratories put it, they "flipped the script for HR." Rather than waiting until they had the perfect solution that was all figured out when they rolled out their talent platform, they told managers that they were experimenting with a new way of working and they wanted to co-create it with them. This got managers involved in owning the solution.

Let Your Pilot Create the Pull

All the organizations we have interviewed and worked with began experimenting with this new way of working by piloting the concept within a few parts of the business first and then, after some initial successes, rolling it out to a broader population. Popular places to start are with IT or product development organizations, or other parts of the business that already operate in more of a project-based workflow. Another common starting point is to work with a function whose business leader has already expressed interest in finding new approaches to fully leverage the talent in the organization.

Many organizations have allowed their full implementation of this new approach to work to grow organically from their pilot. They either adopted approaches similar to those Tata Communications used (asking current participants to leverage their network and invite friends and colleagues to become part of the new Project Marketplace), or they have allowed curiosity and interest to pull people into the network.

Storytelling is another excellent method for gaining interest and enthusiasm for this approach. Success stories captured in vignettes or videos and shared during company meetings, on the platform website and on all types of company communication channels can share the possibilities that this new approach to work holds. Two common story themes have to do with an employee who gained a new skill that enabled them to pivot to pursue a dream job, or a project manager who was desperate for talent and able to quickly find some through the talent platform. At Dolby Laboratories, the company celebrates its Net Talent Exporters by showcasing the stories of managers who are supporting their team members for taking on development assignments outside of their team through their talent platform, Hitch, and celebrating individuals who fully leverage all their skills to contribute to the organization.

Build a Road Map for the Future

If the organization has a significant lack of readiness, it can feel daunting to complete a readiness assessment. But regardless of where you are in terms of readiness, just take one step at a time.

The first time we implemented this new way of working at HERE Technologies, we created a 10-year road map for the future. We knew that some big changes (such as moving from a one-size-fits-all compensation structure to a more agile personalized compensation framework) would take many years to figure out, let alone implement. So we put those changes further out on the timeline—what we expected the workplace to look like in seven to eight years (by 2025). In the near term, we knew we wanted to begin letting people volunteer for projects in parts of the organization that already operated in a project-based manner.

The concept of breaking a job down into projects was not a leap for some parts of the organization, so this is where we wanted to start. But our road map stipulated that within four years, we expected to grow interest in this new way of working and expected more parts of the organization to figure out how to break work into projects. This would enable some significant shifts in talent management practices. In the interim, we developed a plan for new, more agile talent management practices to be introduced to the organization and to use them where they make sense (e.g., feedback at the end of each project, or team members providing input on performance).

Try to envision what the ideal state will look like when the Inside Gig concept is fully realized within a company, and then plan for small steps that, when taken together, will create significant change. You must understand where you are going and what is most important to do first. But you cannot change everything at once; the organization will not be able to absorb all that change.

Change Management Planning

Responsibility for the success of this process must be bestowed upon a single program manager. Organizations that put responsibility for different parts of the process in the hands of different people run the risk of everyone abdicating responsibility and not working together to achieve the company's desired outcomes. While the program manager may also have other related responsibilities (e.g., career development, learning and development, or workforce planning), most companies have invested in a single resource to support this process. This is similar to having one key leader responsible for talent acquisition or performance management.

Beyond the change management steps discussed above (building a business case, gaining management buy-in, defining the road map for success and storytelling), a key role for the program manager is to build momentum for the process. This is often done by identifying a few key influencers in the organization and getting them on board early so that they can become Inside Gig champions and act as ambassadors to the rest of the organization. They spread the word on how the new way of working has benefited them as both individuals and managers.

It is helpful to have well-respected individuals in the company pro-moting this new way of working, but it is critical to align your talent management processes to reinforce and support it. While this will take time, we believe one of the first changes to consider is how you will recognize and reward managers who support this new approach to work. In the case study in chapter 12, we saw how Tata Communications used gamification to draw new participants into the process and to keep them engaged. The more an employee participates in the process, the more points they earn. These points can then be exchanged for access to highly desired learning experiences. This is one approach to incentivize the process. A complementary way to reinforce the process is to include leadership behaviors that support the Inside Gig approach in performance management, compensation and promotion considerations, and succession planning.

However, the most important first step is to design communications for everyone in the organization: employees, managers and business unit leaders. These communications must all reinforce common messages and must explicitly define "What's in it for me?" It is for this reason that each of the chapters in Part Two on the six core principles ends with a section called Perspectives from the Inside Gig. Considering the process from the point of view of the employee, the manager and the company allows an organization to prepare to discuss what's in it for these three important constituents.

Establishing Goals and Metrics for Success

Each company will employ the Inside Gig concept for its own individual reasons. Therefore, we cannot state generally what success looks like. You need to be very clear at the outset of what you are trying to achieve and then articulate your metrics for success. This will help demonstrate the impact and value of this new approach to unleashing the capacity of the organization and creating a process to continuously reskill and upskill the workforce.

Most of the organizations we have studied and worked with have measured the basics:

- Number of unique visitors who have viewed the website

- Number of employees who have created profiles on the platform

- Number of projects completed or in process

- Number of employees who have worked on a project

- Total number or percentage of employees who are active users

Other companies have attempted to assess the increase in workforce capacity by tracking the number of hours contributed on the platform. We are more intrigued by attempts to capture the financial impact of leveraging the company's own talent rather than going outside of the company to hire a freelancer or new employee to do the work, as you saw in the HERE Technologies case study (chapter 12).

Based on the research, we should also expect to see other positive impacts for metrics such as these:

- Increased employee engagement scores

- Reduced turnover rates

- Greater participation in learning and development offerings

- Greater capability to assess the current skills and skill gaps in an organization, thereby helping organization make better data-based decisions for strategic workforce planning

Pitfalls to Avoid

Having worked with and consulted to several organizations implementing project-based opportunity platforms, we can say a company needs some mass to make the system work. With too few people, there are not enough interesting opportunities on the platform to keep interest and activity up. Thus, we recommend not implementing this approach with fewer than 250 full-time employees; 500 would be a safer bet. With more people, you have more skills and capacity to draw from and more projects. HERE Technologies, Dolby and Tata Communications all seeded their systems with interesting opportunities before rolling them out for the first time. This helps to facilitate immediate interest in new opportunities and build momentum for this new approach to talent mobility.

While some companies are beginning to explore how they can integrate this internal talent mobility platform with their external freelance platforms, we have yet to see a way to apply it with hourly employees without a significant amount of hassle and paperwork. So, we do not recommend implementing the Inside Gig with this population of employees.

Finally, do not overcomplicate the process with lots of permissions. We are talking about leveraging people who are already your employees. Less is more. Employing selection processes that mirror your external hiring process will kill this process. We have seen that happen. Limit manager approvals to what is necessary, hold people accountable for doing their job and let them negotiate with their manager how to make room for new project opportunities.

KEY TAKEAWAYS

- Gain management support and buy-in to the process by building a strong business case that employs both external data and data based on company-specific issues (turnover, transitioning skill sets, etc.).

- Assess organizational readiness along four dimensions: mindset; culture; change management; and alignment of the talent operating model, with a specific emphasis on current talent processes. With this knowledge in hand, you can craft specific strategies most appropriate for your company and its stage of maturity to transition to a project-based work environment.

- Determine whether you need to build or buy a technology platform to enable this new way of working. The Inside Gig approach to talent mobility relies on big data and artificial intelligence to facilitate the matching of talent to opportunities and to identify the collective skills of the company.

- Clearly define your new ways of working. Start by getting the management team to agree upon the desired culture and new leadership behaviors that support the process. Management also needs to agree on changes in organizational structures to support the process (e.g., a project management office or new governance structure to manage cross-functional projects). The rules of engagement for the talent platform need to be articulated.

- Start small and use a pilot to learn how to work in this more agile manner, and create pull by letting users speak to the benefits of using the process.

- Share success stories early and often as you employ this way of working. Highlight experiences from different perspectives—employees, managers and the company.

- The change we have discussed here touches every talent process an organization relies upon. It is impossible to change everything at once, so build a road map for a robust change management plan over a long period of time. Look for processes that are misaligned to your new objectives and change them first. As you introduce new changes, always address "What's in it for me?" for all constituents.

Acknowledgments

WE NEED TO START BY THANKING Melinda Merino, editorial director for the Harvard Business Review (HBR) Press. We first approached Melinda with the idea of writing an article for HBR to share the innovative work we were doing in the hopes it would inspire others to change their approach to managing talent. It was Melinda who encouraged us to write a book. She said, "A lot of people have written about various pieces of the story you want to tell, but no one has put it together to create a complete strategy." She told us that to really tell our story, we needed to write a book. The word limitations for an article would not allow us to provide our complete idea. Once we picked our jaws up off the ground, we got excited about writing a book. Thank you, Melinda, for the encouragement!

We could not have written this book without the support, guidance and encouragement of our publisher, LifeTree Media, and especially LifeTree's CEO and publisher, Maggie Langrick, and editorial director, Sarah Brohman. Thank you for the faith you had in these two first-time authors. A special thank you to our editor, Don Loney, for jumping in and making our words come to life (and sound so much better). And to Tilman Lewis, for making sure that we dotted all of our i's and crossed all of our t's. We are also grateful to Laurie Bienstock, Willis Towers Watson, for her thought leadership on the compensation section of chapter 10. Your partnership has been invaluable to us.

While the people mentioned above were indispensable in terms of getting our story written, we need to thank those from whom we got inspiration. To Dr. John Boudreau and Ian Ziskin for fearlessly leading the CHREATE Project (The Global Consortium to Reimagine HR, Employment Alternatives, Talent, and the Enterprise), connecting us with so many amazing CHROs and other HR thought leaders. You pushed us to think harder about the future and create new solutions that would serve the needs of business in the future, not just today. Each and every day you inspired us to think more critically and be more innovative. We especially want to thank Josh Bersin for creating so much thought-provoking research that shaped our thinking and influenced so many, and for agreeing to write the foreword for our book. We could not have asked a more perfect person.

To Eva Sage-Gavin and Marianne Jackson, who invited us to be part of the CHREATE Project, and who also regularly championed both of us. To Edzard Overbeek, who gave Kelley the choice in the work she did and the freedom to pursue a dream, but mostly for being willing to go first and support the idea of creating the Inside Gig at HERE Technologies and then allow us to tell the story to so many other people.

To Aadesh Goyal, Karen May, Christine Landon, George Hudgens, Francine Katsoudas and John Cleveland for so generously sharing their companies' stories with us.

We want to thank Greg Von der Ahe for being such a great thought partner through the years in building out the technology to enable the Inside Gig and for always providing the positive "can do" energy on the mission complete with mindmaps and votes of encouragement. For Deborah Barber, who spent hours giving feedback on early white-board drawings of the talent platform. For Richard Mirabile, Ph.D., for being a sounding board and cheerleader, always believing in this way of working, and lastly, the countless number of HERE Technologies leaders and employees who were willing to be the first adopters of the Inside Gig.

But most of all, we want to thank our families: our husbands, John and Vincent, as well as Kelley's children—Jack, Griffin, Madison and Ella—for their loving support and understanding when our days, evenings and weekends of writing got in the way of some important family time. Without your love, support and encouragement we could never have done this.

Notes

Preface

1. Beverly Kaye, Linda Williams, and Lynn Cowart, *Up Is Not the Only Way: Rethinking Career Mobility* (Oakland, CA: Berrett-Koehler Publishers, 2017).

Introduction

1. See www.CHREATE.net.
2. John Chambers, "How We Did It . . . Cisco's CEO on Staying Ahead of Technology Shifts," *Harvard Business Review* (May 2015): 35–38.
3. Personal communication with Aadesh Goyal, CHRO, Tata Communications, January 6, 2017.
4. Willis Towers Watson, "2016 Global Talent Management and Rewards Study," www.willistowerswatson.com/en/insights/2016/06/2016-global-talent-management-and-rewards-survey-thank-you.
5. Barack Obama, speech, April 2011, Nob Hill Masonic Center, San Francisco, California.

Chapter 1. Disrupting the Talent Operating Model

1. Personal communication with Karen Paul, January 2017.
2. Laszlo Bock, *Work Rules!: Insights from Inside Google That Will Transform How You Live and Lead* (New York: Twelve, 2015), 29.
3. "William McKnight: The Basic Rule of Management That Propelled 3M," Farnam Street blog, September 2015, fs.blog/2015/09/mcknight-3m-management.

Chapter 2. The Fourth Industrial Revolution and Its Impact on Business

1. D'Vera Cohn and Andrea Caumont, "10 Demographic Trends That Are Shaping the U.S. and the World," *Fact Tank: News in the Numbers*, March 31, 2016, Pew Research Center, www.pewresearch.org/fact-tank/2016/03/31/10-demographic-trends-that-are-shaping-the-u-s-and-the-world.
2. Gallup, *How Millennials Want to Work and Live* (2016), www.gallup.com/workplace/238073/millennials-work-live.aspx.
3. Maynard Webb and Carlye Adler, *Rebooting Work: Transform How You Work in the Age of Entrepreneurship* (San Francisco: Jossey-Bass, 2013).
4. Klaus Schwab, *The Fourth Industrial Revolution* (New York: Crown Business, 2017).
5. Till Alexander Leopold, Vesselina Ratcheva and Saadia Zahidi, "The Future of Jobs Report 2018," World Economic Forum, Centre for the New Economy and Society, www3.weforum.org/docs/WEF_Future_of_Jobs_2018.pdf.
6. Douglas Thomas and John Seely Brown, *A New Culture of Learning: Cultivating the Imagination for a World of Constant Change* (Lexington, KY: CreateSpace, 2011).
7. Leopold, Ratcheva and Zahidi, "The Future of Jobs Report 2018."
8. ManpowerGroup, "Skills Revolution 2.0: Robots Need Not Apply; Human Solutions for the Skills Revolution," www.manpowergroup.com/workforce-insights/world-of-work/robots-need-not-apply.
9. Leopold, Ratcheva and Zahidi, "The Future of Jobs Report 2018."
10. Pablo Illanes, Susan Lund, Mona Mourshed, Scott Rutherford and Magnus Tyreman, "Retraining and Reskilling Workers in the Age of Automation," McKinsey & Company, January 2018, www.mckinsey.com/

featured-insights/future-of-work/retraining-and-reskilling-workers-in-the-age-of-automation.

11. Aaron Hurst, *The Purpose Economy*, 2nd ed. (Boise, ID: Elevate, 2016).

12. PwC, "Rethinking HR for the Future of Work," May 2018, www.pwc.com/us/en/hr-management/publications/assets/pwc-saratoga-hr-effectiveness-survey-report.pdf.

13. Leopold, Ratcheva and Zahidi, "The Future of Jobs Report 2018."

14. *Global Human Capital Trends 2016: The New Organization; Different by Design* (New York: Deloitte University Press, 2016), www2.deloitte.com/content/dam/Deloitte/global/Documents/HumanCapital/gx-dup-global-human-capital-trends-2016.pdf.

15. Mercer, *Global Talent Trends 2019: Connectivity in the Human Age*, www.mercer.com/content/dam/mercer/attachments/global/Career/gl-2019-global-talent-trends-study.pdf.

16. Rob Cross, Reb Rebele, and Adam Grant, "Collaborative Overload," *Harvard Business Review* (January–February 2016), hbr.org/2016/01/collaborative-overload.

17. See www.CHREATE.net.

18. Vesselina Ratcheva et al., "Strategies for the New Economy: Skills as the Currency of the Labour Market," January 2019, World Economic Forum in collaboration with Willis Towers Watson, www3.weforum.org/docs/WEF_2019_Strategies_for_the_New_Economy_Skills.pdf.

19. Illanes et al., "Retraining and Reskilling Workers in the Age of Automation."

20. *Global Human Capital Trends 2016.*

21. Bersin by Deloitte proprietary research with Glassdoor, cited in *2017 Deloitte Global Human Capital Trends* (New York: Deloitte University Press, 2017), 29, www2.deloitte.com/content/dam/Deloitte/global/Documents/About-Deloitte/central-europe/ce-global-human-capital-trends.pdf.

22. Benjamin Spar et al., *2018 Workplace Learning Report: The Rise and Responsibility of Talent Development in the New Labor Market*, LinkedIn Learning, www.cornerstoneondemand.com/sites/default/files/partner/asset/files/linkedin-learning-workplace-learning-report-2018.pdf.

23. Accenture Strategy, *Insights from the Accenture Strategy 2016 U.S. College University Graduate Employment Study*, www.accenture.com/t20160512T073844__w__/us-en/_acnmedia/PDF-18/Accenture-Strategy-2016-Grad-Research-

Gig-Experience-Unleash-Talent.pdf; Accenture Strategy, *The Accenture Strategy 2016 U.K. Graduate Employment Study*, www.accenture.com/t20160727T143534 __w__/ca-en/_acnmedia/PDF-25/Accenture-UKGradsSurvey-Classof2016-Infographic.pdf.

24. Mercer, *Global Talent Trends 2019*.

25. Willis Towers Watson, "2016 Global Talent Management and Rewards Study," www.willistowerswatson.com/en/insights/2016/06/2016-global-talent-management-and-rewards-survey-thank-you.

26. Edelman Intelligence, Freelancers Union, and Upwork, "Freelancing in America 2018: 5th Annual Report," fu-web-prod-media.s3.amazonaws.com/content/filer_public/f1/20/f1206c69-0027-4f08-a79a-6877cb90e88a/freelancinginamericareport-2018.pdf.

Chapter 3. Principle No. 1: You Get What You Give

1. Erika Volini et al., *Leading the Social Enterprise—Reinvent with a Human Focus: 2019 Deloitte Global Human Capital Trends*, Deloitte Insights, www2.deloitte.com/insights/us/en/focus/human-capital-trends/2019/leading-social-enterprise.html.

2. Lorrie Lykins and Kevin Martin, *Why Talent Mobility Matters*, Institute for Corporate Productivity, 2016, go.i4cp.com/whytalentmobilitymatters.

3. Volini et al., *Leading the Social Enterprise*.

4. Gallup, *State of the Global Workplace* (New York: Gallup Press, 2017).

5. Edie Goldberg, "The Changing Tides of Careers," *People & Strategy Journal* 35, no. 4 (2013).

6. LinkedIn Talent Solutions, "US Recruiting Trends: 3 Must-Know Talent Acquisition Trends for 2015," 4th Annual Report, LinkedIn, business.linkedin.com/content/dam/business/talent-solutions/global/en_US/c/pdfs/recruiting-trends-us-linkedin-2015.pdf.

7. Anthony J. Rucci, Steven P. Kim, and Richard T. Quinn, "The Employee-Customer-Profit Chain at Sears," *Harvard Business Review*, January–February 1998, 83–97.

Chapter 4. Principle No. 2: Know What You Have

1. Kelly Palmer and David Blake, *The Expertise Economy: How the Smartest Companies Use Learning to Engage, Compete, and Succeed* (Boston, MA: Nicholas Brealey Publishing, 2018).
2. Linda Sharkey and Morag Barrett, *The Future-Proof Workplace* (New Jersey: Wiley Publishing, 2017), 156.
3. "Digital Mobility and Talent Trends," Deloitte, 2017.
4. Dave Ulrich, David Kryscynski, Mike Ulrich and Wayne Brockbank, *Victory through Organization* (New York: McGraw-Hill, 2017).
5. Ellyn Shook and Mark Knickrehm, "Harnessing Revolution: Creating the Future Workforce," Accenture, 2017, 10.
6. Jeff Hesse, "Why Companies Need to Build a Skills Inventory," Strategy + Business blog, October 31, 2017, www.strategy-business.com/blog/Why-Companies-Need-to-Build-a-Skills-Inventory.
7. Emily Ross, Bill Schaninger and Emily Seng Yue, "Right-Skilling for Your Future Workforce," McKinsey report, August 2018.
8. J. Corbin, "State of the American Workplace," Gallup, March 2017.
9. David F. Caldwell and Charles A. O'Reilly III, "Measuring Job-Person Fit with a Profile Comparison Process," *Journal of Applied Psychology* 75, no. 6 (December 1990).
10. "Pulse of Talent: Key Factors for Retaining Top Talent," Ceridian, 2017.
11. Richard Mirabile, Ph.D., "Technology and Intellectual Capital: The New Revolution," *Human Resource Professional* 11, no. 4 (July–August 1998).
12. Dave Carlin and Bill Schaninger, "Matching the Right Talent to the Right Roles," McKinsey report, November 2018.
13. Greg Case, "An Agenda for the Talent First CEO," McKinsey report, 2018.
14. Ross, Schaninger, and Yu, "Right-Skilling for Your Future Workforce."
15. John Pencavel, "The Productivity of Working Hours," *Economic Journal* 125, no. 589 (December 2015).

Chapter 5. Principle No. 3: Create a Learning Organization

1. Volini et al., *Leading the Social Enterprise*.

2. Donald J. Kirkpatrick, "Techniques for Evaluation Training Programs," *Journal of the American Society of Training Directors* 13 (1959).

3. Scott D. Anthony, S. Patrick Viguerie, Evan I. Schwartz and John Van Landeghem, *2018 Corporate Longevity Forecast: Creative Destruction Is Accelerating*, Innosights, www.innosight.com/insight/creative-destruction; "Increasing Churn Rate in the S&P 500: What's the Lifespan of Your Stock?," Seeking Alpha, November 6, 2014, seekingalpha.com/article/2651195-increasing-churn-rate-in-the-s-and-p-500-whats-the-lifespan-of-your-stock.

4. "Reworking the Revolution," Accenture, January 2018.

5. See www.learnabilityquotient.com.

6. Mara Swan, "A Skills Revolution: From Consumers of Work to Builders of Talent," presentation at the HR People + Strategy (HRPS) Annual Conference, 2017.

7. "1900–2000: Changes in Life Expectancy in the United States," Senior Living, www.seniorliving.org/history/1900-2000-changes-life-expectancy-united-states.

8. Lynda Gratton and Andrew Scott, *The 100-Year Life: Living and Working in an Age of Longevity* (Bloomsbury Information, 2016).

9. Carol Dweck, *Mindset: The New Psychology of Success* (Random House, 2007).

10. Personal communication with Karen May, former vice president, People Development, Google, May 22, 2019.

11. Palmer and Blake, *The Expertise Economy*, xxi.

12. https://rework.withgoogle.com/blog/new-guide-employee-to-employee-learning.

13. Personal communication with Karen May, former vice president, People Development, Google, May 22, 2019.

14. "Understanding and Developing Organizational Culture," SHRM, August 13, 2018, www.shrm.org/resourcesandtools/tools-and-samples/toolkits/pages/understandinganddevelopingorganizationalculture.aspx.

15. Palmer and Blake, *The Expertise Economy*.

16. Ellyn Shook and Mark Knickrehm, *Reworking the Revolution* (Accenture, 2017).

17. Daniel H. Pink, *Drive: The Surprising Truth about What Motivates Us* (New York, NY: Riverhead Books, 2011).

18. Benjamin Spar and Colleen Dye, "Linkedin 2018 Workplace Learning Report," learning.linkedin.com/resources/workplace-learning-report-2018.
19. Josh Bersin, "New Research Shows 'Heavy Learners' More Confident, Successful and Happy at Work," Linkedin Learning, November 9, 2018, www.linkedin.com/pulse/want-happy-work-spend-time-learning-josh-bersin.

Chapter 6. Principle No. 4: Democratize the Work

1. Anna Tunkel, "Three Trends on the Future of Work," *Forbes* Business Development Council, August 18, 2018.
2. John Hagel, John Seely Brown and Maggie Wooll, "Can We Realize Untapped Opportunity by Redefining Work?," Deloitte Insights, October 24, 2018.
3. Thomas Oppong, "9 Ideas That Summarise the Future of Work (and How You Can Prepare for It)," *The Startup*, Medium, October 8, 2018, medium.com/swlh/9-ideas-that-summarise-the-future-of-work-and-how-you-can-prepare-for-it-589a985fd642.
4. Irving Wladawsky-Berger, "The Jobs Outlook for 2022," blog post, December 3, 2018, blog.irvingwb.com/blog/2018/12/the-jobs-outlook-for-2022.html.
5. Todd Henry quoted in Oppong, "9 Ideas That Summarise the Future of Work."
6. World Economic Forum, "Strategies for the New Economy: Skills as the Currency for the Labor Market." Center for the New Economy and Society White Paper in collaboration with Willis Towers Watson, January 2019, www3.weforum.org/docs/WEF_2019_Strategies_for_the_New_Economy_Skills.pdf.
7. James Manyika et al., "What the Future of Jobs Will Mean for Jobs, Skills, and Wages," McKinsey & Company, November 2017, www.mckinsey.com/featured-insights/future-of-work/jobs-lost-jobs-gained-what-the-future-of-work-will-mean-for-jobs-skills-and-wages.
8. Sharkey and Barrett, *The Future-Proof Workplace*.
9. Richard Fry, "Millennials Projected to Overtake Baby Boomers as America's Largest Generation," *Fact Tank: News in the Numbers*, Pew Research Center, March 1, 2018.
10. Patricia Buckley and Daniel Bachman, "Meet the Workforce of the Future," *Deloitte Review* 21 (2018).

11. Adam Grant, "What Millennials Really Want Out of Work," Wharton School of Business post, 2015.

12. Jean M. Twenge, Stacy M. Campbell, Brian J. Hoffman and Charles E. Lance, "Generational Differences in Work Values," *Journal of Management* 36, no. 5 (September 2010).

13. Jennifer Deal, *Retiring the Generation Gap* (San Francisco: Josey-Bass, 2007).

14. "Gallup's Perspective on the Gig Economy and Alternative Work Arrangements," Gallup report, 2018.

15. Stan Slap, *Bury My Heart in Conference Room B* (New York: Portfolio, 2010).

16. Hagel, Brown, and Wooll, "Can We Realize Untapped Opportunity by Redefining Work?"

17. Will Begeny and Erin Sheridan, "Impacting Tomorrow's Workforce," Edelman research report, 2019.

18. Gary Hamel and C.K. Prahalad, *Competing for the Future* (Harvard Business Press, 2013).

19. Liraz Margalit, "The Psychology of Choice," *Psychology Today*, October 2014.

20. Anna Bahney, "What Millennials Really Want at Work," CNN Money, December 29, 2017, money.cnn.com/2017/12/29/pf/millennials-work/index.html.

21. *Merriam-Webster's Collegiate Dictionary*, 11th ed. (Springfield, MA: Merriam-Webster, 2012).

22. Sheena Iyengar, *The Art of Choosing* (Arab Scientific Publishers, 2011).

23. Margalit, "The Psychology of Choice."

24. Brandon Rigoni and Amy Adkins, "What Millennials Want from a New Job," *Harvard Business Review*, May 11, 2016.

25. Luis Fernandez, "Guess What, Employees Want Personalization Too," CMS Digital Workplace, April 26, 2017.

26. Olga Mizrahi, *The Gig Is Up* (Austin, TX: Greenleaf Book Group Press, 2018).

27. John Boudreau, "Managing People in a 'Boundary-less' Talent Ecosystem" (Human Resource Executive, 2017).

28. Saadia Zahidi and Vesselina Ratcheva, "Strategies for the New Economy: Skills as the Currency for the Labor Market," World Economic Forum, 2018.

29. Caldwell and O'Reilly, "Measuring Person-Job Fit with a Profile Comparison Process."

Chapter 7. Principle No. 5: Create an Agile Organization

1. Hortense de la Boutetère, Alberto Montagner and Angelika Reich, "Unlocking Success in Digital Transformations," McKinsey & Company, October 2018, www.mckinsey.com/business-functions/organization/our-insights/unlocking-success-in-digital-transformations.
2. George Westerman, "Your Company Doesn't Need a Digital Strategy," *Sloan Management Review* 59, no. 3 (Spring 2018).
3. *Global Human Capital Trends 2016.*

Chapter 8. Principle No. 6: Bust the Functional Silos

1. Laura McPherson, "5 Ways to Break Down Organizational Silos: How to Overcome the Silo Mentality and Encourage Team Collaboration," Zapier, blog post, December 11, 2018, zapier.com/blog/organizational-silos/.
2. Dave Ulrich, Steve Kerr, and Ron Ashkenas, *The GE Work-Out: How to Implement GE's Revolutionary Method for Busting Bureaucracy and Attacking Organizational Problems—Fast!* (New York: McGraw-Hill, 2002).
3. Ron Ashkenas, "Jack Welch's Approach to Breaking Down Silos Still Works," *Harvard Business Review*, September 9, 2015.
4. Tiziana Casciaro, Amy C. Edmondson and Sujin Jang, "Cross-Silo Leadership," *Harvard Business Review* (May–June 2019).
5. Paul Meehan, Darrell Rigby, and Paul Rogers, "Creating and Sustaining a Winning Culture." *Harvard Management Update*, February 27, 2008.
6. Peter Drucker, *Classic Drucker: Essential Wisdom of Peter Drucker from the Pages of Harvard Business Review* (Harvard Business Press, 2006), 3.
7. Leo D'Angelo Fisher, "Can the Silo Mentality Benefit a Business?," *Acuity*, January 12, 2016.
8. "The Changing Role of the Modern Sales Team," SalesForce, www.salesforce.com/hub/sales/how-to-close-the-sale/.
9. "What Is Silo Mentality?," The Perception Game from Perception Dynamics, www.perceptiondynamics.info/silo-mentality/how-to-remove-silo-mentality/.

10. Patrick Lencioni, *Silos, Politics and Turf Wars* (San Francisco: Josey-Bass, 2006), cited in Brent Gleeson, "The Silo Mentality: How to Break Down The Barriers," *Forbes*, October 2, 2013, www.forbes.com/sites/brentgleeson/2013/10/02/the-silo-mentality-how-to-break-down-the-barriers/#3b8358568c7e.

11. "How to Close the Sale: The Changing Role of the Modern Sales Team," Salesforce, www.salesforce.com/products/sales-cloud/resources/breaking-the-silo-mentality/.

12. John Nemo, "What a NASA Janitor Can Teach Us about Living a Bigger Life," *The Business Journals*, December 23, 2014.

13. McPherson, "5 Ways to Break Down Organizational Silos."

14. Casciaro, Edmondson, and Jang, "Cross-Silo Leadership."

15. Morten Hansen, *Collaboration: How Leaders Avoid the Traps, Build Common Ground, and Reap Big Results* (Boston: Harvard Business Review Press, 2009).

16. Joan Gallos, *Organization Development: A Jossey-Bass Reader* (San Francisco: Jossey-Bass, 2006), 565.

17. Michael I. Norton, Daniel Mochon, and Dan Ariely, "The 'IKEA Effect': When Labor Leads to Love," Harvard Business School working paper 11-091, 2011.

18. Phred Dvorak, "How Understanding the 'Why' of Decisions Matters," *Wall Street Journal*, March 19, 2007.

Chapter 9. A New Talent Operating Model: Rethinking Ways of Working

1. Karen Stephenson, "Neither Hierarchy nor Network: An Argument for Heterarchy," *People + Strategy Journal* 32, no. 1 (2009): 4–7.

2. John Boudreau, Ravin Jesuthasan, and David Creelman, *Lead the Work: Navigating a World Beyond Employment* (Hoboken, NJ: John Wiley & Sons, 2015).

Chapter 10: A New Talent Operating Model: Capability Alignment

1. Amy Edmondson, "Psychological Safety and Learning Behavior in Work Teams," *Administrative Science Quarterly* 44, no. 2 (June 1999).

2. This section was coauthored with Laurie Bienstock, Willis Towers Watson. Laurie Bienstock would like to acknowledge the Talent and Reward Practitioners at Willis Towers Watson—partners in forging the path forward for Work and Rewards.

3. John N. Bremen and Amy DeVylder Levanat, "The Future Is Now: Work and Rewards in Evolved Organizations," *Workspan* (March 2018): 45.

Chapter 11: A New Talent Platform: Taking an Idea from Concept to Action

1. John Boudreau, Carolyn Lavelle Rearick, and Ian Ziskin, eds., *Black Holes and White Spaces: Reimagining the Future of Work & HR with the CHREATE Project* (Washington, DC: Society for Human Resource Management, 2018).

Bibliography

Aghina, Wouter, Karin Ahlback, Aaron De Smet, Gerald Lackey, Michael Lurie, Monica Murarka and Christopher Handscomb. "The Five Trademarks of Agile Organizations." McKinsey Report, January 2018. www.mckinsey.com/business-functions/organization/our-insights/the-five-trademarks-of-agile-organizations.

Arena, Michael J. *Adaptive Space: How GM and Other Companies Are Positively Disrupting Themselves and Transforming into Agile Organizations.* New York: McGraw-Hill, 2018.

Blenko, Marcia, Eric Garton, and Ludovica Mottura. "Winning Operating Models That Convert Strategy to Results." Bain & Company, December 10, 2014. www.bain.com/insights/winning-operating-models-that-convert-strategy-to-results/.

Boudreau, John, Carolyn Lavelle Rearick, and Ian Ziskin, eds. *Black Holes and White Spaces: Reimagining the Future of Work & HR with the CHREATE Project.* Washington, DC: Society for Human Resource Management, 2018.

Cowgill, Bo, and Rembrand Koning. *Matching Markets for Googlers*. Boston: Harvard Business School, 2018.

De Smet, Aaron, and Chris Gagnon. "Organizing for the Age of Uncertainty." McKinsey Quarterly, January 2018.

Dhawan, Erica, and Saj-Nicole Joni. *Get Big Things Done: The Power of Connectional Intelligence*. New York: Palgrave Macmillan, 2015.

Goler, Lori, Janelle Gale, Brynn Harrington, and Adam Grant. "The 3 Things Employees Really Want: Career, Community, Cause." *Harvard Business Review*, February 20, 2018. hbr.org/2018/02/people-want-3-things-from-work-but-most-companies-are-built-around-only-one.

Romansky, Lauren. "Ease Your Talent Crunch by Building a Vibrant Internal Labor Market." Human Resource Executive, April 18, 2019. hrexecutive.com/ease-your-talent-crunch-by-building-a-vibrant-internal-labor-market/.

Meister, Jeanne C., and Kevin J. Mulcahy. *The Future Workplace Experience: 10 Rules for Mastering Disruption in Recruiting and Engaging Employees*. New York: McGraw-Hill Education, 2017.

Sloman, Colin, and Robert J. Thomas. "Humanizing Work through Digital." Accenture Strategy, 2016.

Sullivan, John. "Managers Are Hoarding Talent: A Hidden Problem That's Likely Hurting Your Firm." TLNT, September 25, 2017. www.tlnt.com/talent-hoarding-a-hidden-problem-thats-likely-hurting-your-firm/.

Index

About the Authors

Edie Goldberg, PhD, is the president of E.L. Goldberg & Associates in Menlo Park, California. She is a nationally recognized expert in talent management and organization development. Her practice focuses on designing human resources processes and programs to attract, engage, develop and retain employees. Dr. Goldberg has published and presented at numerous conferences on the future of work, performance management, building management capability, career management and succession planning. She earned her doctorate in industrial/organizational psychology from the University at Albany, SUNY. Currently, she serves on the board of directors of the SHRM Foundation; she is the past chair of HR People + Strategy (HRPS) and past-president of the California HR Strategy Forum (HRSF). She is the recipient of the HRPS Lifetime Achievement award to honor the impact she has made to her profession.

Kelley Steven-Waiss serves as CHRO of HERE Technologies and is the founder of Hitch. She has been a CHRO in technology for the last 12 years, with more than 25 years of executive management and consulting experience in human resources, change management and corporate communications. Currently, she serves on the board of directors of FormFactor, Inc. (FORM), a publicly traded semiconductor company based in Livermore, California, and is the advisor board chair for Silicon Valley Education Foundation (SVEF). She earned her BA in Journalism from the University of Arizona and her MA in HROD from the University of San Francisco. She has been recognized by *WomenInc.* magazine as one of 2019's Most Influential Corporate Directors. She is married with four children.